THE NORFOLK LIBRARY

Within Living Memory

Other titles in the Norfolk Library

ALAN SAVORY: Norfolk Fowler
ELIZABETH HARLAND: No Halt at Sunset

Within Living Memory

A collection of Norfolk reminiscences
written and compiled by members
of the Norfolk Federation of Women's Institutes

THE BOYDELL PRESS · IPSWICH · 1973

Published by The Boydell Press Ltd
PO Box 24 · Ipswich IP1 1JJ · Suffolk

First published 1972
Norfolk Library edition 1973

Text design by Don Parkinson
Illustrations by M. F. Peck

Printed in Great Britain by
Redwood Press Limited
Trowbridge, Wiltshire

ISBN 0 85115 030 6 (hardback)
ISBN 0 85115 033 0 (paperback)

Contents

Foreword

The pace of change in everyday life has never been so swift. Familiar objects become obsolete, life long habits inappropriate, almost overnight. This can be stimulating; it can also be unnerving. It is probably more necessary than ever before, that people should have a sense of continuity in the midst of change. One of the most satisfying ways of doing this is to look back, as readers of this book are invited to do, to the different pattern of life experienced by Norfolk women who have lived on into a world where they can see, on a television screen, men walking on the moon. They have lived through a social and cultural revolution, but they have not been overwhelmed by it; their personalities have not been eroded nor their integrity impaired; they are the living links between the old world and the new.

The small precise details which build up a picture of a vanished way of life are preserved in the memories of ordinary men and women. It is of vital importance, not only to the professional historian, but to every thinking person, that this oral tradition should be preserved, as it is so vividly, sometimes so movingly, in this book.

Rachel Young
Assistant Director, Norwich Museums

Preface

History is what happened yesterday, not just in the big headlines, the big events, and to important people, but also to ordinary people in their everyday lives.

Most of us begin to realise that our yesterdays have become history when things which seem unnoteworthy and commonplace to us become interesting curiosities to our children. 'Tell me about when you were young,' must have been said by child to mother from generation to generation, and if only, over the centuries, mothers had written down what they told their children, the social historians of today would have had a goldmine of first-hand information.

To help historians of the future—and for our own enjoyment and interest—we have tried in this book to present a composite picture of the commonplace things of everyday life in the Norfolk countryside over the past ninety years, as people still alive today remember them. It has been compiled from essays entitled 'I remember . . .' written by members of the Norfolk Federation of Women's Institutes for a European Conservation Year competition in 1970.

We are not presumptuous enough to claim originality for this idea of recording immediate past history while it is still in living memory. We know that others more skilled and learned than ourselves are actively working in the same field. We do not claim to have unearthed hitherto unknown facts of social history, nor are we trying to draw conclusions from the facts presented. We simply present this composite picture, drawn directly from the memory's eye of a number of people who have lived through the same period of time in different parts of Norfolk, in the hope that it will not only give pleasure to both old and young, but will also add some more living colours to the overall picture of this period of English life.

Perhaps all the same we can claim that the colours in our picture have some special quality not found in all other collections of reminiscences by virtue of their being mainly women's memories at a time when men and women's spheres of activities were more sharply distinguished than they are today. And rural women's reminiscences of this period, in a sparsely populated big county such as Norfolk must inevitably be different in many ways from those of townswomen.

It is undoubtedly an intensely interesting period of rural life to record, a period during which the pattern of country life was being changed beyond all recognition by the coming of farm machinery, modern transport and electricity. Many of the contributors to this book have lived in Norfolk, and sometimes in the same village, all their lives. They have been part of this revolution in the same surroundings, so that the contrast between present and past is all the more vivid and personal.

The Norfolk Federation of Women's Institutes itself has lived through more than half a century of the changing country pattern, and indeed has played its part in bringing about the change, as Institute and County Federation records show. Here certainly is more fascinating material to be written up one day, but for the present we leave our members to speak for themselves in this collection of memories.

We are grateful to all those who provided material for the book: their names are listed on Page 155. To our regret we were not able to include extracts from all the essays submitted, as it would have meant some duplication of material, but all the contributions, without exception, were of value in deciding on the shape and content of the book.

We would also like to thank Miss Rachel Young, Deputy Director of Norwich Museums, and Professor W. G. Hoskins of Exeter for their help and advice, the Centre of East Anglian Studies at the University of East Anglia for help with manuscript copying, the Women's Institutes' volunteer typists for preparing the book for print, Miss Marion Peck for the illustrations, and Mr Don Parkinson of Norwich City College for the design and typography.

Zita James
County Chairman
Norfolk Federation of Women's Institutes

Part One

Domestic Life

**Food and Drink   Putting down the pig   Washday   The Chores
No mod cons   Callers at the door   The end of the working week**

Food and Drink

Men, remembering their youth, think nostalgically of the meals that mother produced, of all the things that made home feel like home.
Women think of these things too, but because like their mothers they have probably been cooking and home-making for as long as they can remember, their memories search back curiously to find out how mother did it.
Take away the gas, the electricity, the piped water, the mechanical aids, the cars and buses for getting to shops, the tinned and frozen foods—in fact all the things that we find essential for feeding the family, how *did* they manage?

No oven Blakeney 1890's

On Saturdays you would see housewives carrying their joints of meat to the bakeries to be baked in the large ovens. Many cottages in those days had no means of cooking a joint.

The wall oven Great Moulton 1930's

On baking days the little fire was lit under the wall oven in preparation for a batch of cooking. A wall oven cooked well, but it had to be fed with sticks or coal, and many a time I remember the oven fire dying down at the most awkward moment, causing the pastry bowl to be left in order that more fuel could be collected for the fire.
But my mouth waters as I think of the lovely rabbit pies my mother used to make in this oven. She would prepare two rabbits and put them in a huge pie dish, make a crust, decorate it with pastry leaves and pop it in the oven. We usually had this cold the next day when the removal of the crust would reveal a layer of lovely jelly.

Baking Day Spooner Row 1910

Every Friday was baking day, and all was done in an oven in the wall, heated by coal. We children were sent to the farm about half a mile away with a large can for one pennyworth of skimmed milk, and woe betide us if we had spilt any on the way home.

The country kitchen Sandringham 1920

How the women managed in those days I can't think, but I remember the wonderful Norfolk dumplings like snowballs that Mother made, home-killed and home-cured pork, and meat rolls that Father called 'four horse rolls' because they were so big. These were eaten in the kitchen with its shining cooking range, well scrubbed red tiles, a lovely warm piece rug on the hearth, and always a Norwich canary hanging in the window.

Home-made, home-produced (i) Bunwell 1906

When we were children, my sister and I were often sent to spend part of the long summer holidays at Bunwell in Norfolk with an elderly couple whom we called Uncle Lambert and Aunt Gussie but whom we now know to have been our Great Aunt and Great Uncle.

Our uncle was a wheelwright, and his cream painted house with its steep, thatched roof stood some fifty yards back from the road. The grass to the right of the broad driveway was kept short by the pecking of Auntie's plump brown hens, which provided all the eggs for the house.

All water was drawn from the well or from an enormous rain-water butt which drained the roofs of the forge and the paint shop. Cooking was done on two hobs over the open fire or in the oven built into the wall beside the fireplace and heated from below by its own small fire of twigs and wood. Looking back on those days from the standpoint of our own domestic amenities, constant hot water to which we give not a thought and electric cookers which we can set to cook a meal and to switch themselves off at the appropriate time, I marvel at the memory of the lovely meals, the bread, pastries and cakes which came so perfectly cooked out of that primitive oven in the wall.

Auntie used to summon us for 'elevenses' by a shrill blast blown on a small horn whistle which hung beside the house door. Sometimes she would produce a small oval cut-glass dish and send us to a neighbouring farm for half a pound of home-made butter or a honeycomb.

(ii) Swanton Novers 1910

I was born in 1901 in a very old cottage with oak beams and a huge fireplace, which was flanked by an oven in the wall, where the twice-weekly batch of bread was baked.
My Dad worked in a railway works two miles away, and we had one acre of garden so that he and my Mother spent every spare minute working in it. She planted all the seeds and managed the cucumber frames. I remember that one rather poor and large family always sent on Sundays for a halfpenny cucumber, which Mother interpreted as all the curly mis-shapen ones.
The garden provided us with fruit and vegetables but my Mother also sold fruit and flowers to supplement the family income, and many were the young men who came on Sunday morning for a buttonhole, a favourite being a bud of the 'Gloire de Dijon' which grew on the wall.

Harvestfield Dinners (i) Neatishead 1930

At harvest-time I sometimes used to stay at my grandad's farm in the next village. What a business it was taking dinners and teas into the cornfields! Not for them neat parcels of sandwiches and cakes; these were considered snacks to be eaten at 'elevenses' and 'fourses'; and so, as a child, I helped to carry baskets with hot rabbit pies or steak and kidney puddings, basins of hot potatoes, with jam puffs or apple pie, all covered with white cloths. My grandmother provided dinner for the men at harvest time and they would sit round the spread out food, knives and forks would be handed out and everyone would tuck in to a good substantial meal, washed down with tea or, for those who preferred it, something stronger out of stone jars kept in the shade of the hedge.

(ii) Horningtoft 1890

I was sent with my grandfather's dinner to his harvest field. We looked in the basket, and as it looked good we ate some, then went a little further and sat down and ate it all, went to the field and stood the basket inside the gate and ran home, and did not say what we had done. My grandfather came home and said to grandmother, 'Why did you send me empty dishes?'

(iii) Shotesham 1900

At harvest time I would help one of my sisters take my father's dinner into the harvest field. Mother would let us take our dinners too. Sometimes she would make meat dumplings. There would be a large one for my father and two smaller ones for us. They were boiled in a cloth. There would be very little meat in ours but I still think they were the nicest dumplings I have ever had.

Home-brewed beer (i) Very potent Swanton Novers 1910

Mother also brewed beer, very potent I believe, but I liked it only when it was new and sweet; also elderberry wine, very spicy, hot and with a piece of toast. It was very soothing when one had a cold.

(ii) Not so strong Drayton 1910

Granny used to brew home-made beer. It couldn't have been very strong as I once drank half a bottle and filled it up with cold tea and my grandfather didn't notice.

The food that was free (i) Nature's bounty Strumpshaw 1920

All the food that was for free: watercress from running streams, rabbits, pigeons, wild raspberries, wild plums and blackberries, crab apples, hazel nuts, chestnuts, walnuts. No squirrels hoarded these more carefully than we did. Skim milk free for the fetching—

far superior to today's pinta. A god-mother who kept bees and had all the children in to help scrape out the sections. Apples and pears that were laid out, in the order they had to be eaten, in the spare room, to see us through the winter.

(ii) The farmer's bounty Knapton 1880's

My mother used to go gleaning in the fields when we were young and get enough corn to take to the mill to be ground into flour for bread to last the year through.

(iii) Straight from the hedges Shipdham 1917

We ate blackberries and other delicacies straight from the fields and hedges and consoled ourselves that everyone ate a peck of dirt before they died. We knew where all the best chestnut and walnut trees were and rubbed our fingers nearly raw to remove the tell-tale stain before going to school.

(iv) Rabbits and long-tailed pigeons Drayton 1910

There were lots of rabbits about, and the banks were honeycombed with warrens. Good dinners they made. I suppose they damaged the crops then but the men round that way used to go rabbiting and kept them within limits. Everything was well organised when they went rabbiting. They took ferrets and nets to put over the holes and long-handled diggers. Some of the men used to go out at night with long nets. I believe they used to get pheasants in them but I wasn't supposed to know. Any birds we ever had to eat were called pigeons even if they were not.

The food you paid for Saxlingham 1890

Butter from the farm was only tenpence a pound, and eggs one shilling a score—not a dozen. Milk we got for three halfpennies a pint, also collected from the farm and we paid a penny for three pints of skim milk separated by hand which left a good percentage of cream in the milk, and what delicious milk puddings it made. Bread was twopence halfpenny a two pound loaf.

Putting down the pig

Mrs Beeton fastidiously disapproved of the pig when alive, but fully approved of him dead: 'Setting his coarse feeding and slovenly habits out of question, there is no domestic animal so profitable or so useful to man as the much maligned pig, or any that yields him a more varied or more luxurious repast'.
But perhaps Mrs Beeton never had a family pig who became a family friend, and so was not torn between sorrow at the friend's undignified and untimely end, and pleasure at the wonderful enrichment of the diet that followed his death.

At the Manor House Blakeney 1890

One of my recollections at the Manor House which is not so pleasant is the putting down of a pig. After being killed and cut into joints the pig was brought into the kitchen and all had to help with the putting down. I can still feel the cold of the raw meat as we cut it up for sausages, pork cheeses and so on. The hams and chaps were pickled in large lead pans in the dairy, and when ready, taken to Mr Alcock the carpenter's shop where they were hung over the smouldering woodchips to be smoked. They then came back to be hung up in white bags on the kitchen beams until they were wanted to be eaten—and how good they tasted!

One got rather tired of pig Swanton Novers 1910

My parents also kept hens and pigs, and one of the occasions of the year was pig-killing time. The big copper was filled and boiled up, and the local pig killer came trundling a sort of wooden stretcher, with handles at each end, on one iron wheel. On top was a big wooden tub, called a 'killer', with all the tools of his trade. The pig having met his end, came the task of removing all the hair from his hide by means of hot (not boiling) water, and sharp scrapers. He was then cut open and hung up till the next day. Then our man returned to cut him up, and I had the job of carrying various joints to friends and neighbours.
Mother salted the hams and later sent them to be cured. She also

made pork pies, chitterlings and pork cheeses, till one got rather tired of pig at last.

Our poor pet pig Shotesham 1900

We had a large garden and my father would grow all the vegetables we needed to help to get extra money. He also kept pigs and when they were ready to be killed the butcher would come and slaughter them on the premises. How I hated it! If we were not at school, my sisters and I would run a long way from the house. If it was wet we would shut ourselves in a cupboard and block our ears. When it was killed our poor pig would hang up in our living room, from a big hook that was in a beam, in the middle of the room. I had to go past it to go to bed and it would take a lot of courage for me to go. Our next door neighbour would come in and say to me: 'You silly great Mawther—it on't hart you, it's dead'. It wasn't hurting me that worried me; it was because while the pigs were alive they were our pets. I can remember one of them eating one of my straw hats.

There would be plenty to eat at that time. My mother would make lard and we would have pig's fry and sausages and pork cheese. The neighbours would also have some of the meat and the butcher would take the remainder to sell at his shop.

Oak smoked hams Foulsham 1920

Pig killing time was always looked forward to as there were lovely tasty dishes to eat after this—pork pies, scraps, pork cheeses and pork—*all pork*—sausages. Some of the pork was put into brine, salt enough to float an egg. We had boiled pork and onion dumplings. After the sides and legs of the pig had been in the brine long enough they were taken to our local fishman who cured them for us in his curing shed over oak smoke. The hams today never taste anything like they did.

Washday

Memories of food are mainly happy ones and it is even possible to think that the food was better and tasted better in those days. But nobody sheds tears over the passing of old-fashioned wash-days. It all took such a time, with so much toil for the sake of cleanliness!

Sweet Smells Shipdham 1920

The weekly wash was done every Monday and seemed to last all day. Anything that would burn was saved for the copper fire and whatever the season of the year, the air was 'sweet' with the smell of burning rag and old boots. The copper itself was filled with rain water (caught off the wash house roof). Sometimes it was green and smelly and sometimes full of squiggly things.

Extra Hands Blakeney 1890

Monday was a great day at the Manor House as our extra helper came in and she and the two maids retired to the big laundry to do an enormous wash. They then carried all the linen out to the Sand Hills (now the Caravan Site) singing as they went along with their big baskets. Next day all the ironing was done with flat irons, or box irons heated on a very antique stove in the middle of the laundry.

Hateful Monday Great Moulton 1930

One thing I did not like was wash day. I hated Monday. The copper fire was lit early, and then a ritual of soaking, washing, starching, rinsing and boiling commenced. The kitchen was soon full of bowls, tubs, baths and steam, and my mother was lost in misty clouds, or up to her elbows in soap suds, rubbing away till I thought her fingers would soon show the bones. This wasn't the end, for on Tuesday came the ironing.

The fire had to be made up and burning clearly for the metals from the box iron to be heated. One was placed carefully into the iron with the fire tongs, down went the iron's shutter like a guillotine, and it was ready for use. It was a very heavy iron to use and noisy too as the metal inside hit the sides of the box. The flat iron was not much easier to use as this had to be heated on the oil stove or on the fire and it was put in a chromium holder. Both sorts of iron were very fond of making sooty marks on the clothes if one was not careful.

The Box Mangle at the Pub Southrepps 1880's

My mother, now aged ninety-eight, can remember going with her mother to mangle linen in the Long Room situated at the back of the public house which was known as The New Inn, now a private residence known as Ham House. This mangle consisted of a huge box of large stones collected from the beach, and was worked with a large handle which, fastened to a large roller, propelled the box of stones back and forth. A charge of twopence was paid to the owner.

The Chores

It must have been worthwhile to be rich in those days, if endless cleaning, polishing and sewing were not to your taste. Unlike today, with plastics, stainless steel and permanent polish for all, the hardworking housewife used once to be clearly distinguishable from the lazy one by the amount of shine in the house.
And in our day, with no lamps to be kept well oiled, the wise and the foolish virgins are indistinguishable.

Helping Mother Shipdham 1920

On Saturday morning we children each had our own special job to do. Pocket money had to be earned. I had a steel fender and fire irons to clean with emery cloth and how I loathed the sight of that fender! But tears and skinned knuckles didn't help and got me nowhere. There were also knives to be cleaned on a board, spoons and forks cleaned with whitening and shoes cleaned with blacking. Blacking was a solid concoction in a tin (costing one penny) which had to be dampened before use, so you spat in it if no one was looking.

Six Maids Drayton 1910

My grandfather, with whom I lived, was gardener to a gentleman in Drayton. There were about six maids kept at this gentleman's house. Wages were low and most of the village girls went into service. There were no labour-saving devices then: steel fenders and fire irons and copper pans were used and needed endless cleaning.

The long winter evenings Reedham 1910

My granny used to do all the sewing in the winter time, making my grandfather shirts, flannel nightshirts and all my underwear too. We children used to make rag rugs ready for the next year's spring cleaning.

Oil Lamps Great Moulton 1940's

Oil lamps and candles provided us with light. These had to be kept clean and the lamps filled with oil. During World War Two a friend of the family recommended some black tablets to help make the oil used in the lamps more efficient. My mother had a packet of these in a drawer in the kitchen. My father, who loves sweets, pounced on them one day thinking he had found a secret store. One taste was enough, and the first we knew of all this was when we found him gargling and rinsing his mouth out.

Tallow Dips Mulbarton 1910

At my grandfather's farm at Mulbarton, where we stayed as children, grandmother made clothes and knitted stockings for her family of eight, made preserves, pickles, butter and tallow dips for lighting.

Sorting Feathers Sandringham 1920

When I was a small child, if it was wet when we visited my grandmother we helped to sort and cut feathers for feather beds. No wild birds' feathers were put in, especially not wild ducks or geese. These would make you want to wander, she would say.

No mod cons

The petty at the end of the garden and water from a well are not by any standards, old or new, convenient. But in some people's memories they seem to be part of a lost country idyll. Perhaps both provided an unassailable excuse for escaping from the family, or from some unpleasant chore, from time to time.

The Teamsman's Home Shotesham 1900

We lived at Shotesham and my father was teamsman on a farm on the estate of the late Robert Fellowes.
My parents worked very hard. My mother would make my father's shirts, and the younger children's clothes, sewing them by hand and, in the winter, with only a light from a paraffin lamp.
There was no fresh water at the cottages. It was brought twice a week by horse and cart in milk churns and it was stored in large earthenware pots in the pantry. It had to be used very sparingly for cooking and drinking.
Water for washing the clothes and linen was obtained from a large pit, and for bathing, rain water was stored in large tubs. Sometimes my father had to bring water from the farm in two pails hung from a yoke from his shoulder.

Progress from wells to village pump Aylsham 1913

On 29th May, 1913, the village pump was opened. I was sent on an errand but found myself at the opening, hoping to get at least one of the pennies which were to be thrown to the children. I was not disappointed for I did get one, and a scolding too into the bargain when I arrived home.

Distance lends enchantment Strumpshaw 1920

No modern conveniences—but who cared? The joy of a bath in front of a blazing fire with lots of soft water in the winter-time, what bliss! The petty down the garden path: a beauty spot in spring and summer but quite an adventure in the dark evenings with a flickering candle lantern.

The Petty and the Well Shipdham 1917

I remember as a child in 1917 coming to live in Shipdham. I was born and lived for the first years of my life in London. There were five of us. Three cousins, my sister and I, and I was the eldest. The village was five miles from the nearest railway station and I remember the pony and trap that met the train and the jog-trots through the country lanes in October sunshine, to the cottages which were to be our future home. The hedges high on either side were bright with autumn leaves and berries and I thought: 'These are mine for the picking; no notices saying "Please keep off the grass" and no dire penalties for picking flowers.'

The cottages (we filled two) had thatched roofs, beamed ceilings and brick floors. Across a yard was a wash-house and at the bottom of a very long garden there was what was always referred to as the 'Petty'. In the Petty, side by side at different levels were two well worn seats with lids on—a large one and a small one, and I well remember that first winter how we escorted each other down that long garden path after dark, with a candle in a lantern which we stood on the seat between us, usually after an argument as to who should occupy which. We were never alone, for the largest spider ever hatched had been in residence long before 'The Squatters' came. We were very brave until the wind blew the candle out, or an owl hooted in the trees near by. Then we would run like mad back to the house leaving a sister or cousin stuck on the Petty yelling her head off.

It seemed we had left one danger behind us, (the Zeppelin raids on London), only to have many more perils to contend with.

Our drinking water came from a well in the garden. We brought it up with a bucket and chain, icy cold and crystal clear and drank it as it was with no ill effects. Pollution was something you looked for in the dictionary! There was no refuse collection, so everybody burned their rubbish.

The Town Cousins' View of the Country (i) Horstead 1910

My early days were spent in Norwich, and my first holiday away from home began with a ride in a carrier's cart. I was delivered to the carrier's care in an inn yard, deposited among the packages and parcels, and trundled along the country roads at a rousing five miles per hour. Arriving at the 'Recruiting Sergeant', I was duly handed over to my aunt and cousins to begin a brief, but strange and thrilling sojourn in the country. Clear in my memory still is the wooden hut in the garden, with primitive toilet arrangements (to accommodate two at a time) and the ever present fear that I might fall through!
Then the joy of cranking the bucket down into the mysterious depths of the well, and the icy first drink from it.

(ii) Blofield Corner 1910

We watched with awe when we saw water being drawn from the well. This was a serious business and we were warned not to climb or play around it. The warning was unnecessary as far as I was concerned, as I felt frightened on hearing a clanging sound as the pail swung further and further into the deep dark well. The clear fresh water, however, was nice to drink and although we would not admit it, we did agree with Fred when he said 'Somethin' different to your ol' tap wa'er'.

Polluting the Precious Water Foulsham 1920

Our water had to be drawn from a well and the boy on the farm used to draw some buckets of water every morning before going to his other jobs. One day I was in sad disgrace as I had been given a clay pipe with which to blow bubbles and somehow managed to make all the water soapy. I never forgot how angry auntie was but I suppose she had to wait until someone came home at dinner time to get her some fresh water.

The house in the woods Kelling Heath 1930's

Being a mere 38-year-old, I must seem a youngster compared with some of our senior citizens writing their memoirs, but I have the advantage of being a pure-bred 'Norfolk Swede', with past generations scattered in church-yards all over Norfolk. My maternal grandmother could even remember the building of the Sheringham to Norwich railway line which was one of the miracles of her generation.

I was the third daughter of a Norfolk game-keeper and was born in a primitive, isolated cottage on the edge of the beautiful Kelling Heath near miles of densely covered woodlands. Acres upon acres of trees of all varieties just beckoning their leafy branches to three small children to play in their sheltering arms. From my point of view they more than made up for the dark, damp and dismal house that could only have been designed by a member of the opposite sex. Tiny little windows deliberately closing their eyes to the fairy-tale view outside, with a puny north-facing kitchen with at least eight doors each letting in its separate gale to our frozen feet. Drinking water was drawn twice-daily by Father from a sixty foot well, which was still the mode used by most of the villagers, as I remember that a long row of council-houses had to share one well between all of them and it provided a meeting place for the men to chat. Rain water from the water butts was used sparingly for washing and bathing purposes. In the summer droughts all water was brought from the well on Sunday night for Monday's wash-day. If the chain broke, dropping the bucket to the bottom of the well, there was a mammoth fishing expedition with a hook on the end of a line.

The only cooking facilities were an open grate in the kitchen which was always surrounded by heavy iron-bottomed saucepans and the baking was done in an oven-in-the-wall variety which my poor Mum battled with once weekly. It had all the vagaries of an ageing spinster, waiting patiently till it received the fruit cake before either dropping the temperature to zero or blazing fiercely to singe the edges and afterwards winking its big brass eye at us.

Of course we had paraffin lamps in the living room and candles for bed-time with many a book read at night by the light of a smuggled candle. All nocturnal trips to the outside lavatory (which stood like a sentry box about 100 yards from the house) were accompanied by a dear old tilly lamp. We all three used to go together, quite an expedition with us all donning wellington boots and macks in wet weather.

Callers at the door

You could indeed be self-contained in your village, before the days of cars and buses: what you could not produce or make yourself, was likely to be brought to your door by travelling tradesmen. Now you probably fetch it yourself from a self-service shop, so which way is progress? But the tramps who called at the door have gone, and that *is* progress.

Pedlars Wood Norton 1910

Travelling pedlars regularly visited Wood Norton. One old man came driving a donkey cart, with clean silver sea sand which he sold to housewives for scouring pots and doorsteps and for spreading on the brick floors. There was the oil-man who sold paraffin for the domestic lamps—electricity in the village was still twenty years in the future—and who always asked: 'Which will ya hev, the best or the cheap?' On being told the 'best', he would say: 'Ah ma-am, the best *is* the best', and disappear behind his cart to draw the oil from the one and only tap. Unfortunately, my father-in-law, who one day was quietly gardening behind the hedge, observed this strategem and enquired from where he drew his cheap oil?
Another visitor was the rabbit-skin man, bearing on his shoulder a long stick on which were skewered numerous rabbit skins, purchased at the cottage doors for twopence apiece, a thriving trade in the years before myxomatosis had ever been heard of.

The Tinker Shipdham 1920

Our nearest neighbour was a tinker and scissor grinder who also did some poaching to supplement his income. He would sally forth with his barrow to neighbouring villages where he mended pots and pans and sharpened knives and scissors. His barrow was a wonderful affair with a seat where he sat and pedalled to make various wheels go round. When he soldered kettles there were loud hisses and horrible smells. Getting closer than I should one day and commenting on the nasty smell, he informed me it was 'camels urine'. On another occasion he extracted from a capacious pocket a pretty bird with a long tail and putting his finger to his lips he said 'Sh! Sh! that's a Japanese Peacock!'

He was a good neighbour in times of trouble and when the oven or copper wouldn't draw he would oblige with a charge of gunpowder up the chimney. If pigs from 'The Hall' trespassed on to his or neighbours' gardens he would load his gun with dried peas and those pigs literally flew back. We rather enjoyed this interlude in our young lives. The old man's language wasn't very choice but as he stuttered rather badly the full impact seldom reached us.

Milk, Turnip-tops and Fresh Fish Aylsham 1910

All sorts of people came to the door. Milk was delivered by a schoolboy, carrying two pails slung from a wooden yoke across his shoulders. It was ladled into jugs on the door step. A little girl, in a long tattered dress, with unkempt hair, brought something green in a small basket. It took my parents several weeks to understand her broad Norfolk 'Tarnup tops—Salus, threepence a barskit!'

There was a fisherman who came regularly each week by carrier cart from Sheringham. He carried a basket on each arm filled with fresh fish and crabs, lobsters and shrimps when in season. He gradually became a personal friend, chiefly because my mother, (Lowestoft born and bred) knew good fish when she saw it, and was able to clean and fillet her own purchases.

Tramps came regularly, and were always given a jug of tea and something to eat. Their grapevine kept them coming!

Milk from the Churn Spooner Row 1910

Our milk was from a churn brought round by pony cart. People brought their jugs to the door to be filled from the tap of the churn in half pint or one pint measures.

The Coal Cart Saxlingham 1890

I am now living in the little cottage I was born in in 1886. I can remember Queen Victoria reigning, so you see I have seen six different sovereigns in my lifetime of eighty-four years. I can remember when coal was tenpence a hundredweight delivered by horse and cart from Wells, about eleven miles away.

The Cockle Cart Sandringham 1920

The cockle carts came on Saturday mornings. We always had hot cockles or mussels for Saturday tea, winkles on Sunday, and samphire in season.

Tramps Neatishead 1930

In those days it wasn't unusual to see tramps on the road, making their way from one workhouse to the next (roadsters they were called locally). These 'gentlemen of the road' would often call at houses along the way and in return for bread and cheese, cake and a mug of tea or cocoa would chop wood or maybe dig a strip of garden.

Tramps and Lost Travellers Matlaske 1910

Snowy winter mornings would bring shivering tramps to our door. They had slept rough, on their way from workhouse to workhouse. When my mother struck a match to light a fire in the polished grate, grimy hands, blue with cold, would stretch out to it: 'Aah tha's bettah'.

Our school and house stood in an isolated lonely spot. My father kept a cudgel by the front door. Often benighted travellers with horse and trap, lost in our narrow roads, would knock to be directed on their way. My brother would stand behind the door and open sharply while my father stood with his bullseye lantern in his left hand and his cudgel in his right.

The end of the working week

Bathrooms, the National Health Service, the five-day working week, and the disappearance of strict Sundays have reduced the significance that Saturday night used to have with its important rituals of personal cleaning-up, both inside and out, in readiness for the solemn rituals of Sunday.
But children undoubtedly like ritual, and with more frequent baths and less purges now, they will probably remember some other weekly landmarks of their childhood when they are old.

The Docile Children Reedham 1910

Saturday night was bath night. The copper would be filled with soft water and we would be bathed in a tin bath in front of the fire in the winter time but out in the wash house during the summer months.
Another weekly feature was the dose of sulphur and treacle that my grannie used to mix up and we swallowed down. We even got to like it. In any case there was never any question about taking it.

The Cunning Ones (i) Shipdham 1917

Saturday night was bath night and once more the copper was filled with rain water. The water was heated and carried across the yard to a tin bath in front of the kitchen fire. In we all went one after another, starting with the youngest and finishing with me. Carbolic soap gave 'the richest and creamiest lather'. It also killed all 'known and unknown germs'. I don't remember the water being changed but I do remember it being topped up with more hot water dipped out of the copper with a hand cup (a metal bowl with a wooden handle). We cleaned our teeth with carbolic tooth powder (fourpence a tin). After the bath—the purge! Liquorice powder and how I hated that stuff! My little sister was partial to it, and so obligingly drank mine as well as her own, (if no one was looking). On Sunday dressed in our best clothes we were clean inside and out but some were cleaner than others.

(ii) Drayton 1910

On Saturday nights I used to be dosed with liquorice powder which I detested and gave to the dog if no one was looking. He liked it and didn't suffer any ill effects as far as I know.

Curls for Sunday Strumpshaw 1920

Long hair was marvellous, plaited in two long plaits tied with an enormous bow. But on Saturday evenings the same hair would be wound up tightly in rags to have curls on Sunday—ugh! To this very day I hate curls.

Part Two

Pleasures & Pains

Children's Pleasures   What we wore   Medicine and Magic
Leisure

Children's Pleasures

The moral of all these reminiscences of children's pleasures seems to be that the toy-making industry could disappear completely without any loss of happiness in the world. Every modern mother knows well that her child is as happy with a discarded cardboard box as with the most sophisticated spaceman.

But of course it was country children who used to have the advantage when it came to making their own toys and amusements; there was nature's bounty and plenty of space, on the door step. And throughout these tales of childhood stands out the theme of the now lost for ever peace of the roads. 'We played our games on the road undisturbed apart from an occasional horse and cart . . .'

Childhood Games Spooner Row 1910

I was born and brought up in the Norfolk village of Spooner Row in an age when the pace was so much slower than today. No wireless or television—in my case just a phonograph for pleasure which my father operated. My sister and I used to be delighted when the box of tube-like records of old songs and ditties was brought out and played to us.

We seemed to enjoy life to the full with so many make-believe games as well as bowling hoops, spinning tops, playing hopscotch and marbles and five stones, all done on the roads, or sides of roads, as there were no playing fields available. It was great fun seeing who could keep a top spinning the longest with a whip and father was often putting new hob nails in the base of our tops which he had shaped from large cotton reels, or of course more elaborate ones could be bought.

In the autumn the pop gun was greatly used and prized. There was always the hunt for a thick piece of elder wood about nine inches long. We scooped all the pith from the centre to make the barrel after which we put half an acorn in each end. Then a firm piece of stick to push (from one's chest) from one end to the other to make a loud pop.

Another game we were fond of was leap frog or jump back as we called it when three or four of us would travel quite a way in this fashion on the grass at the side of the road. I belonged to two organisations, The Girl Guides and the Girl's Friendly Society. Some of the Guide meetings were at the village school and some at Wattlefield Hall, the home of the Captain who was Mrs Routh Clarke, the founder President in 1918, of our Women's Institute. The GFS meetings were held at Morley Hall at the home of the late Miss Hill and there we learnt the finer points of sewing and embroidery.

We had social evenings occasionally at the school, and I particularly remember going to one in a fancy dress I had made to represent a game called Put and Take. This game was played with a small metal six-sided top to be spun on the table, and I have this small object in my possession now, and also some of the wooden spinning tops.

My favourite sweets from the local shops were, I remember, flat sugar sweets with short messages from Cupid on them, and monkey tobacco, which was coconut shreds coated with chocolate and sherbet. Sherbet was a yellow powder with a sharp bitter-sweet taste. A penny was a treasure to take to the shop as it would buy four separate items.

All children had to walk to school, some as far as three miles and it was usual for those of us who lived near the school to leave home early and meet our friends from further away. Sweet chestnuts which we picked up on the way during autumn were treasured in pockets to be traded later for perhaps a coloured glass marble and little boys quarrelled for acorns and conkers. Parents had no need to fear for their children's safety from traffic on the roads. Winter evenings were spent by the light of the oil lamp, knitting, crocheting and making dolls' clothes, and summer evenings outdoors, when fine, skipping and playing hopscotch. When out to play on Saturdays and school holidays we used to know the time by the the trains: 'I reckon that's the quarter to five: it must be nearly tea time'; and if we were anywhere near the railway gates we always climbed high and waved to the engine driver and his mate who both always looked very sun-tanned with a cap on their heads and an oily rag in their hands.

The Large Family Runhall 1890's

I was born at Runhall in the reign of Queen Victoria, in a row of farmworkers' cottages. Most of them had large families. There were seven of us, five boys and two girls. My two eldest brothers were in the Norfolk Regiment. They came home on leave looking very smart in their uniforms. They wore navy trousers, scarlet tunics with brass buttons and a white belt, a small cap with a Britannia badge on it. It was quite a performance, cleaning buttons and badges every day. The belt with cleaned with pipeclay. We girls spent hours making chains of daisies, cowslips, primroses, buttercups and dandelions.

We fetched our milk from a farm in a tin boiler: four pints of skim milk for a penny. To reach the farm, we walked up a lane which had a deep ditch on one side. There we found primroses, violets, cowslips and every kind of wild flower. Best of all, we found lovely wild strawberries. These we picked and strung on a long stem of grass. Then we would sit down and eat them.

The only traffic along our road was the baker's, butcher's and grocer's carts, so it was quite safe for us to play our games in the road. We had great fun with skipping, hopscotch, marbles and fivestones. We had a hoop of either wood or iron to run along the road with a stick. My favourite toy was a popgun. One could buy them but we had very little pocket money, so my brothers made them from an alder stick with the pith removed. A hazel nut stick would make the other part. Our ammunition was an acorn, or a ball of wet newspaper. When discharged they made a lovely 'pop'.

Valentine's Day (i) Runhall 1890's

We looked forward each year to Valentine's day. When it got dark the older boys would go outside, lay something on the door-step, give a loud knock and run away. When we opened the door, we found the various gifts, a new hair ribbon, elastic garters, pencils, crayons, and other things. When the gifts were finished, the boys would play a joke on us. They would tie an apple or an orange to a piece of string, lay it on the doorstep and knock. When we tried to pick it up, they snatched it away.

(ii) Griston 1920

On Valentine's day, the village children came to the door and sang:

'Good morrow Valentine,
God bless the Baker
You'll be the giver
I'll be the taker'

They were then given pennies and apples.

(iii) Burgh St Peter 1880

We used to start Valentine's Day on February 14th by getting up at six o'clock in the morning, and going to the Rectory and farm-houses shouting 'Good morning, Valentine, draw up your window blind'. They would give us some pennies. Some we had to scramble for. We used to finish up at the village shop and buy some marbles. I always longed for a monkey-on-a-stick.

Holiday Pleasures Sprowston 1910

The summer holidays were eagerly awaited each year, as there was always plenty to do. Many days were spent gleaning in the corn-fields. I also helped to pick fruit and a little later would go acorn gathering. A farmer nearby would pay a few coppers for a pailful of acorns for food for his pigs and he also bought the corn from gleaning for his chickens.
As a child I was very happy improvising games although there seemed to be special games for each month of the year—marbles, hop-scotch, five-stones, hoops, skipping, diabolo, tip-cat, to mention a few. Also we used to make daisy chains, beechnut necklaces, little baskets from stalks of wild grass and perfume bags from muslin and lavender.

Beating the Keepers Swanton Novers 1910

Around our village were large woods where lilies of the valley grew. We were allowed tickets to go and gather them. But to us children it was much more exciting to sneak in and snatch a handful before the Keepers caught us.

Pocket Money (i) Shotesham 1900

Sometimes I would have a farthing to spend on sweets, or cushies, as they were called by my grandmother.

(ii) Saxlingham 1885

My pocket money when I was a child was one penny per week, that is if I hadn't been naughty. We had a little shop in the village in a back room of one of the cottages where our pennies used to be spent. How delicious those sweets were coming from a glass jar, not wrapped of course, and given to us in a screw of newspaper—unhygienic perhaps, but we survived.

Winter and Summer on the Broads Filby 1897

I do not expect many people have both rowed and walked across Filby Broad. It was 1897 and I was a girl of eight. After a very severe winter all the Broads in East Norfolk were frozen over for six weeks and I can remember going to Sunday School and my mother meeting me and taking me over the ice.
I had been taught to row before then, my father had his own boats and we were all taught to row, but I can remember my sister and myself getting stuck in the mud.

The Seasons' Joys Strumpshaw 1920

I remember with nostalgia my very happy childhood half a century ago in a quiet Norfolk village, in an old farm house surrounded by fields and woods, a Broad and a river nearby which meant a boat and always dogs. Each month of the year had its delights.

January and February with dykes and marshes frozen solid, the thrill of being able to slide to school, and one never-to-be-forgotten occasion when the whole school played truant. Our formidable head mistress joined us, on skates, and treated us to an awe-inspiring display of figure skating.

March and April brought out our spinning tops, skipping ropes, hoops, marbles and five-stones. No cars on the road, so one could have great fun whipping a top or skipping to school.

May and June were interesting months when we found bird nests and watched progress. There was great competition to find the first flowers. Haymaking too in the fields—hay in cocks was a wonderful place to play hide-and-seek in.

July and August brought school holidays and harvest. My father was a gamekeeper so did not 'do' harvest but I took a neighbour's dinner and 'fourses' every day and my own of course. Food never tastes so good as in a harvest field. In the summer too, trips on the river. Rowing a boat came naturally and we watched the Norfolk wherries transporting goods to Norwich. In August came Mum and Dad's yearly holiday, a long day at Yarmouth catching the earliest possible train, stopping on the way down to the beach for bread rolls, (shame on us for enjoying them so after home made bread) butter, ham, and cheese and fruit. Then paddling all day—a trip out to Scroby—up to the promenade late in the afternoon to buy hot freshly boiled shrimps, fourpence a pint in those days, and more rolls for tea. What did it matter if a little sand did get mixed in? Finally tired out, very happy, catching a train home always with a box of Yarmouth bloaters. I never remember it raining.

September and October were the golden months picking up acorns for a farmer who kept pigs and paid so much a bushel. The joy of earning some money, when a penny went a long way.

November brought bonfire and fireworks. A huge bonfire of bracken and hedge trimmings, always a straw guy, but we rushed to get safely indoors before the fireworks went off.

December brought birthday and Christmas with parties, Sunday school parties in particular, with Christmas Tree and a present for everyone.

Birds' Nests and Ruins Kelling Heath 1930

One of the family rules I hated most was having to wear Wellington boots for our summer jaunts across the heath owing to the numerous adders basking in the sun. We were not afraid of them as they usually slithered away in the opposite direction at our approach. I even saw one coiled up in the flower beds in the garden one warm day. Birds-nesting was a favourite pastime in the spring and we found several quite rare nests that would probably delight ornithologists. It was fashionable then to collect birds' eggs, and I am now ashamed to say I had quite a remarkable collection; it is a hobby which I would not encourage my children to begin.

With great reluctance I must confess to another game which archaeologists would call desecration. We had a fairy-tale castle ruin where we used to clamber up the crumbling walls, slipping and slithering down again bringing down large chunks of falling masonry with us. It is now quite a famous building owned by the National Trust known as Baconsthorpe Castle, but it was a secret then between us and many wild birds. My father climbed up to the top of it when he was a boy to collect the eggs of a kestrel which had nested in its top-most pinnacle. It even had its original drawbridge then which had disappeared before the National Trust took over.

Oak Apple Day (i) Matlaske 1910

I remember 29th May, Oak Apple Day. When I was about eight years old, my boy sweetheart left home early on that morning to bring me a sprig of oak. I had jobs to do before I left the house, and I had no time to get oak. But the little lad was always there to supply me with the sprig, to save me from the 'pinch' given to any without oak that day.

(ii) Aylsham 1910

'Twenty-ninth May is Oak-apple Day
If you don't give us a holiday
We'll all run away'

We used to sing this and wear a sprig of oak on the twenty-ninth of May, and after meeting in the playground with our Union Jacks we would go to Church and in the afternoon have sports. The last Oak-apple Day I remember was when Mr George Wones walked round the town carrying a large branch of oak, bearing a placard 'Oak-apple Day is dead' and a big black bow.

When cars and planes were rare Neatishead 1930.

When a local farmer bought a motor car, it was a contraption to be watched right out of sight. But one car in the village wasn't much of a hindrance to our bowling hoops and spinning tops along the roads.
How exciting it was to hear the drone of an aeroplane, and we would stop whatever we were doing, to scan the skies for a sight of a tiny plane.

Granny's Tales Sandringham 1920

Seabirds over the marshes at Wolferton are what I love most to remember and the tales told me by my grandmother of smugglers hiding kegs of rum in her parents' water butt. She also told many tales of haunted farm houses she had lived in. I loved these in the day time but at night I wasn't so sure.

The Backward Village Shipdham 1910

When I went from Norwich to stay at Shipdham I took my diabolo with me and found I was quite a sensation when I played with it in the village, as this new-fangled thing had not arrived there as yet.

Concert by Lamplight Bunwell 1906

In the evening, when the tablecloth had been removed and dusk began to fall, Uncle would place the oil-lamp in the centre of the table, remove the white glass shade and proceed with the ritual of lighting it. We were little town girls accustomed first to gas and later to electric lighting and this paraffin lamp fascinated us. Under its mellow light we played dominoes until bedtime. Sometimes we gave a concert, songs, duets and items from Uncle on his concertina.

Dolls, and Piglets from Heaven Drayton 1910

In Norwich we liked to look at the shops in the arcade. There was a lovely toy shop there and I always admired the doll's prams but they were always too expensive for me to have one. I had a doll's pushchair though and numerous dolls: a wax one whose face all melted when I left her in the sun and ones with china faces and a jointed wooden one with black hair painted on; these were called Dutch Dolls and made in all sizes. The dolls of today are so much prettier and made of stuff that doesn't break if they are dropped. Many tears were shed over broken dolls in my youth.

We had a sow called Sally who was almost a pet and had many litters of dear little pigs. What pretty creatures they were and how pleased I was when my Grandfather took me to see them! I thought they had dropped from Heaven as I had no idea about biology then, either animal or human. Perhaps I was dim or stupid but anyway I wasn't a dunce at school.

I hope I haven't given the impression that we were poor and dismal. I had a happy childhood and although I didn't have lots of toys we had marvellous games of 'let's pretend'. I believe on the whole people were more contented and that was a great gift.

No Pram for the Doll Horningtoft 1890

I was always fond of dolls. I had a wooden one with a painted face and black hair. It was a favourite and I dragged it on a bough to school, as I did not possess a doll's pram.

Larking in the Reading Room Mulbarton 1880's

'In our village', the old man said, 'we had a reading room; but the only paper I ever see'd was the E.D.P., I used to get it myself from X and take it down as soon as the room opened. We boys had fun and games there. One thing I remember was to pull a heel iron

from our boots, put it into the fire, and when we heard the gates we'd get it out and throw it in the middle of the floor. Time and time again it would be picked up and dropped with a yell. The caretaker lived next-door and she used to make tea, coffee or cocoa at a penny a cup. Three of us boys would go regular like and say—"Cup of tea please"—"Cup of coffee please"—"Cup of cocoa please". She'd get real mad and say "Can't you boys have the same?" "No ma'am," we'd say, 'We wants different". She'd be that mad, her wig would slip up and down—that's true it did, and didn't we boys laugh?'
'Do you look back with pleasure to those days?' I asked my old friend. 'I do, I do' he said with conviction. 'We were poor but we had love. We made our own amusements. We worked hard and had few presents. We were content.'

The Maypole and the Mighty Empire Shipdham 1917

I remember dancing round the Maypole on the village green on May Day in a white embroidered dress (bloomers underneath). We played our games on the road undisturbed apart from an occasional horse and cart or a drover driving cattle to market. We were told that ours was a great country with a mighty empire upon which the sun never set, and we nearly burst with pride when we sang 'Land of Hope and Glory' and other patriotic songs on Empire Day.

What we wore

Comfort and convenience seem rarely, throughout the centuries, to have been a deciding factor in shaping clothes. Even now, to be fashionable often means to be uncomfortable.
But unlike their great-grandparents when young, at least the children of today are allowed to be comfortable in their clothes, and grandmothers are not expected to dress as though they were a hundred.
Boots and their discomforts loom large in these memories of childhood, as they often did as a worrying item in the family budget. The inventor of rubber boots deserves a high place in the ranks of benefactors of the human race.

No Rubber Boots Wood Norton 1910

Among some of the discomforts of his Norfolk childhood my husband remembers the hard wooden pressure of leather, when, in the days before the advent of rubber boots, children's snow-soaked footwear had to be dried making it very uncomfortable till the leather softened.

Boots for the Teamsman's family Shotesham 1900

Often at night after he had had his tea, Father would mend our boots, 'high lows,' he would call them. Our boots had to be very strong as we had a lot of walking to do.
Although we had to wear each other's left off garments my mother would not let us wear each other's shoes. A shoemaker would come out to measure us for our boots.

Clothes for School South Creake 1913

In those days boys wore stiff white Eton collars, Norfolk jackets, corduroy breeches which fastened at the knee, over long woollen stockings (and reeked abominably). Their leather boots had steel tips, clates, and hobnails all over the sole, and they could strike sparks from the flints on the rough roads.

The girls wore white pinafores over their dresses, long woollen stockings, and boots of a lighter make than their brothers.
I remember that I trudged along in black buttoned boots, and wore a crimson coat with a shoulder cape and bonnet to match. When I was in haste, the velvet strings on the bonnet would always tangle, and my frantic efforts to untie them would result in tears by no means silent, or restrained—a noise which my teacher compared with the bellowing of a bull.

Envy Drayton 1912

We all wore strong lace up boots—how I longed for fancy shoes! All the girls wore white starched pinafores to go to school. Some of the girls wore velvet dresses which I always envied.

Sunday Best (i) Shotesham 1900

When my youngest sister was born, I became the middle one of five girls. It had its advantages and also its disadvantages, as although I did not have to help with the household chores, neither did I have the new clothes, but had to wear those my two elder sisters had outgrown. The day came when my mother said she would take me to the dressmaker for a fitting for a new dress. I was fascinated when I got there. I had never seen so many pins, they were everywhere.
After the fitting, which was done very thoroughly, I was given the task of picking up the pins, whilst my mother chatted with the dressmaker.
How proud I was when I got my new dress and wore it for Sunday school with a new straw hat trimmed with daisies. Most of the little girls wore hats like it in those days.

(ii) Bunwell 1906

Uncle was 'chapel' and Auntie was 'church' so, in our best silk or voile dresses and our flowery leghorn hats, we accompanied Uncle to chapel in the morning on Sundays, and walked with Auntie over the fields to church in the evening. As we walked, my great-aunt's long dress of frilled black taffeta with yoke of jet beading and lace, made a gentle swishing sound—to me it seemed the height of elegance.

(iii) Great Moulton 1930

I well remember watching my grandmother getting ready to walk the two miles to the other side of the village to church. After putting on her best black silk dress and black hat, coat and gloves, she would get a large white handkerchief out of a box on her dressing table, and sprinkle it liberally with lavender water. Then, having collected her hymn and prayer books, hooked her brolly on her arm, and tied her collection up in the corner of her handkerchief, she was ready to set off. She always allowed plenty of time so that we did not have to 'gallop' as she put it.

Curls for the Outing Horstead 1910

In these days of hair-styling and permanent waving, one looks back with a smile to the days when we girls would arrive at school with hair twisted into strips of rag or paper to produce cork-screw curls when going to the annual Sunday School treat. This was a feature, not discouraged by the teacher, which always announced to the less fortunate that a treat was in store for those thus adorned.

Very Old at Sixty-five Norwich 1910

Into the cab got my mother, three children and granny, possibly only sixty-five but dressed in the fashion of those days: black dress, cape and bonnet, with feathers (violets and sequins for high days). She looked at least a hundred years old compared with the grandmas of today.

Clothes for Work (i) Burgh St. Peter 1890

My grandfather was dressed in a long-sleeved fustian waistcoat, brown duffel trousers, and black wide-awake hat. In my memory I

can see him going up and down the field with a pair of dibbles, and my granny walked behind dropping potatoes in the holes.
When I was fourteen I started service. I wanted to be a teacher, but at the time of the examination which I should have taken, I had an attack of quinsies. My mother prepared my clothes, three of everything. I had print dresses for mornings, and black dress for the afternoon, made out of my granny's cashmere shawl. I had aprons, caps, petticoats, bodices, and one dress for best. There was not much opportunity to wear it.

(ii) Swanton Novers 1900's

Our woods were reckoned to be the best haunt for woodcock in the country, and King Edward VII came to shoot often. I never saw him, but I remember the Keepers in green frock-coats with bright buttons, and the Beaters in smocks.
I also remember going to church in a white frock with a black sash, on the day of the King's funeral.

Medicine and Magic

Diphtheria to mothers today is a word only known when combined with 'immunisation against,' but it is only since the Second World War that it has ceased to be a dreaded killer. So many fears of illness and its results used to lurk in the shadows, with no wonder drugs, no health service and no sickness benefit. But perhaps with camphorated oil, boiled onions, or vinegar and brown paper the lesser illnesses went away just as fast as they do today—and at least the remedies didn't make things worse.

Mother knew what to do Rollesby 1900

'What did you do when you were ill?' I asked the old man. This question only produced a puzzled look.
'Well, I remember I had diphtheria when I was eight, and the doctor came three times one Sunday. He gave me up. After that I never was ill. Mother knew what to do for us children, and the Village Nurse came in when my brothers and sisters were born.'

Illness meant Disaster Waxham 1900

In 1900 we moved from Filby to Waxham to a much larger farm, then trouble started. The farm was bounded on one side by sea, bleak and cold; my father lost four horses one week, then foot and mouth disease broke out among the cattle, and there was no compensation. To crown all, father was very ill for a year, then all the family had diphtheria and the water was condemned.
In those days there were no butchers, bakers or deliveries of groceries; you even had to fetch your own doctor.

Boiled Onions and Camphorated Oil Strumpshaw 1920

Colds and sore throats had their brighter side—no tablets or injections. A fire in the bedroom made up for the indignity of flannel soaked in camphorated oil; there was hot onion gruel or boiled onions literally floating in butter, and we were allowed to read in bed.

Rubbing Salt in the Wound Matlaske 1910

Once a harvester came at twilight for first aid. He had not heard the boy holler 'Holdjer', and a pitch fork had pierced his hand as he caught at sheaves being tossed into the waggon. My father washed the wound and filled it with salt. How that man danced round our kitchen! My father hastily sent me away out of earshot.

Tiz for Tired Feet Drayton 1910

I don't remember aspirins and such tablets being about then. Beechams Pills were. I used to have Cod Liver Oil and Malt from Boots. It was quite cheap. Camphorated Oil was rubbed on chests for colds and there were some lozenges called Peps. Tiz was good for tired feet—you put it in the water. My grandfather swallowed a couple of these once, he thought they were pills.

Vinegar and Brown Paper Mulbarton 1880

'My dear mother' said the old man, 'she suffered cruel from head aches, and in them days, there was no running off to surgeries—not that there was time for it anyways, but as I was saying, she was laid low for two or three days with these bad heads, and I spent my time dipping brown paper into vinegar, and laying it on her forehead. 'Ah' she'd say 'That's lovely, boy!'

Tonsils on the Doctor's Table Fakenham 1910

An icy wind was blowing over Fakenham Heath one March morning nearly sixty years ago, as a horse and cart was driven briskly along the stony road. On the floor of the cart, covered with a warm rug, crouched my husband then a small child. Earlier in the day his father had driven him seven miles to Fakenham from his home at Wood Norton. There, on the table in the doctor's surgery, his tonsils had been removed and he was now returning home, where his mother would put him to bed and nurse him until his throat was healed. He remembers this journey vividly.

Superstitions Wood Norton 1910

Superstition and belief in folk-lore were very common, especially among the older people. After a sow had farrowed it was customary to hang the after-birth on either an apple tree or a blackthorn—'so that the pigs do well,' and my husband saw his grandfather take down his gun to shoot a cuckoo which was cuckooing down the chimney when his grandmother lay ill, as he believed this was a sign of coming death. On summer nights after dusk, the children would avoid a boggy meadow where the ghostly 'Lantern Man' ran about with his blue lights, and as they had never been told that it was only the marsh gas burning, they were afraid. Boys believed that if they took eggs from a robin's nest the one who did it would subsequently break his offending arm, and as this actually happened to one child, that surely was proof enough!

My husband's cousin, who lived in another North Norfolk village, used to tell him of an elderly brother with his two sisters who kept bees in the old-type straw hives. They would talk to the bees and tell them not to go away and hive, and thank them for a busy day's work. When the honey was ready the sisters made mead, and from the honeycomb beeswax, which was sold to tailors to wax their threads. The brother died, and the sisters at once draped the hives in black crepe and informed the bees when the funeral would take place. After the funeral, which they described to the bees, part of the crepe was removed. The remainder was cut off gradually during the next three weeks, and when all was gone the bees were told to start working again. It was believed by many people that if these rites were not performed the bees would all die.

My husband also speaks of the 'tinging' of the swarming bees, when the veiled owner would follow a swarm, 'tinging' by making a noise with two metal objects, so that when it eventually settled he could rightfully claim it. The old sexton's wife always used a stout iron dust-pan and the huge church key for greater efficiency.

Leisure

Norfolk schoolchildren today go on educational cruises in the Mediterranean, school parties to Paris, skiing holidays in the Alps. For many of the older generation, an organised outing in their youth meant a journey of a few miles, in a cleaned-up coal cart or beribboned farm wagon for an afternoon's fun and games in a field, or, for the really lucky ones, at the seaside.
One sociologist's worry of today used not to exist for most working families: the problem of leisure activities. No leisure—no problem. But there were the occasional high days and holidays, the visits of fairs, coronations, jubilees and the like, which stand out like beacons by their rarity.

Not much Leisure Norwich 1910

My life as a child sounds ridiculous to my grand-children and others of this modern age. The average working man had only two days holiday: one Christmas Day and the other August Monday, so the highlights of a child's life were a trip to Yarmouth, a ride on top of the tram to Mousehold and the annual Sunday School outing—mostly in a coal cart!

The Chapel Anniversary (i) Swanton Novers 1905

I belonged to Church, and our Summer Treat was a trip to Sheringham, in old Sam's Waggonette and two horses. But I always felt a bit envious of the Chapel children at Anniversary time. A Barn was decorated with bracken and flowers, and the children were on a waggon with the Harmonium, which our Rector's wife played on that day, and no Church services were held. All the girls had new dresses, and each child had its own moment of glory, when even the smallest had a verse or a few lines of 'piece' to say. The elder ones of course had long poems to recite. The following day they paraded the village in the waggon singing hymns, till the Chapel was reached, where they had tea. Later all went to the recreation ground, to scramble for nuts and sweets. I was not allowed to go until my Mother was sure that was over, in case I, a Church child, got one! But I enjoyed the singing games which followed, traditionally the last was 'kiss in the ring'. This is the last verse of one:

Now you are married, you must be good,
And help your wife to chop the wood,
Chop it fine and carry it in,
And kiss each other in the ring.

(ii) Wood Norton 1910

Chapel would also provide the Anniversary, when two farm wagons, drawn up end to end in a large barn, would be decked with bluebells and gorse. In them the Sunday School children, the girls in new dresses and with hair curled and beribboned, and the boys in best suits bright with buttonholes, would stand and sing. My husband, who could be trusted not to forget his words, was charged with the recital of the all-important 'Collection Piece'. If not enough money to take these dear little children to the seaside was forthcoming, the performance was repeated and the hat passed round again, and indeed the reward was well deserved, for there had been many weeks of rehearsal before the Great Day when the procession was formed on the village green and wended its way, singing hymns, to the barn, a full mile distant.

Sunday School Treats (i) Sprowston 1910

Our Annual Sunday School treat was looked forward to with great delight, and near to the day we kept our fingers crossed for fine weather. This was a very special treat and I can remember having a new dress for the occasion each year. All the children had to be at the church at about half past one. Farmers lent out their waggons for us to ride in. Some of the waggons had forms put in, so that the children could sit, but in some waggons the children had to kneel or stand. The horses were of the heavy type and did not run, just plodded along, and we were told to be careful not to frighten them when waving the flags which we had been given, near their heads. We sang and cheered all the way to Sprowston

Hall Park and tumbled out of the waggons to chase around, compete in the many races, and also try out the swings. At about five o'clock we had tea, usually consisting of gooseberries or strawberries to eat with our bread and butter and lots of sticky buns.

After tea the prizes were given for the races and then it was time for our return. Three cheers were given for the Squire and off again to another hilarious ride.

(ii) Aylsham to Cromer 1910

Oh those Sunday School treats to Cromer! We travelled in wagons lent by local farmers who also provided the horses and the drivers. By seven-thirty in the morning we were at the loading point. There were no late risers on that day. We had our lunch and tea at Cromer on a meadow near Coln Cottage—strangely enough I never remember a wet day for our treat—then back home, but not too tired to try to scare some of the other children with kitty-witches.

I remember one year my eldest brother went on such a treat and on arriving at Cromer bought a picture postcard and posted it to my mother. It was to let her know that he had arrived safely and the weather was fine. The card reached my mother by the afternoon post (yes, you may remember we had three deliveries a day then.) My mother treasured this card and I still have it among my odds and ends for I am a real hoarder.

A Little Love and Religion Gimingham 1920

Our old Rector, 'Uncle', as we called him affectionately, was born a hundred and twenty years ago. He died at eighty, having served our village for forty years.

Every summer there was a booking which Tammy the cabman never forgot. This was to take dear old Uncle to the station for the annual outing to Yarmouth. It was a real village outing financed by Uncle, and one which he enjoyed as much as anybody. Practically everybody was eligible in some way. The men's club, the choir (the same thing as a rule), all the school children and toddlers, and the Mothers Meeting Members.

This was a gathering which met periodically to drink tea, sew and be read to. My mother often did the reading. When asked how she chose suitable books, I remember her saying in her very practical way, 'Oh, those which have a little love and religion in them.'

The children began to congregate in the Grove, hours before they were due to start. For many of the little ones it might be the first ride in the train, but for all it was a red letter day. The children were taken to the station in farm waggons, and when these turned into the Grove they always cheered and shouted. Loading processes took some time, small children were lifted in and told where to sit, and given injunctions about leaning over the side. Boys clambered up the wheels, and those who had been hanging about in the hope of riding one of the horses were pushed up and told to mind what they were about. When everything had been settled to the satisfaction of the schoolmistress and the men in charge of the waggons, the procession started, waggons first, with one or two bicycles as sort of out riders. There was a good selection of prams and pushcarts following full of toddlers and a few babies with mums anxious to make a day of it too. Lastly with great dignity came Tammy with Uncle and the Headmistress in the cab, the Junior having been loaded into the waggon to keep an eye on the children. At the station Uncle had a sixpence ready for every child to spend, and he also provided a slap up tea for the whole party. A generous, lonely old man he loved taking out his flock, which was to him his family.

The Brewery Outing (i) To our Village Mulbarton 1890

'Did I ever tell you about the Brewer's annual trip? Well, it happened this way,' said the old man. 'Every year in summer—and bless me if I ever remember a rainy day—along came the Brewer's men, their wives and their children. They came from the town to our village, the horses would be dressed up with plumes and ribbons, and all the people in their Sunday best—the boys did stay home from school to watch the fun. As soon as the cavalcade arrived, the horses would be taken to the stables, and the people would all make for the pub. They'd have a dinner there, and boy what a dinner! and speechifying of course. Then on to the Common for Sports. My! didn't I love the barrel-rolling—I never missed that. Those men who were going in for the race would gather at a certain place, then at the word 'Go' they'd roll those barrels at a spanking pace—just using one hand to keep the thing a-rolling. It was a great sight for us boys. When it began to grow dark, the horses would be harnessed, to the drays, and off they'd go at a fine trot, the women holding torches aloft. Many's the time I've followed them most of the way back to the town.

(ii) From our Town Norwich 1900

My father was a drayman at a brewery and I remember seeing a photograph of a brewery outing with my mother looking years younger than I could ever remember her, with a very smart hat on. I am sure it must have been one which my elder sisters had given her; she would never have been able to afford such a hat. The workers used to travel in waggonettes and usually stopped for a meal. In the front of this photograph were large musical instruments so I guess they had music as they travelled.

Cricket, and Flower Shows Swanton Novers 1910

We were two-and-a-half miles from a station and a very quiet village, but there was a flourishing cricket team, my Dad being their star bowler. Their big day was Whit-Monday, when the match was between the married and single men of the village, so nearly all the folk had an interest in one side or other.
Another occasion was August Monday, when a big flower show was held in the neighbouring park. My parents would be up most of the previous night, washing and preparing vegetables, arranging collections of all sorts, and flowers. There was a class for children, usually a darn on canvas, or a buttonhole on calico. I don't remember ever gaining a prize, but each competitor had a free entry ticket so that meant twopence to spend on halfpenny ice cream, or rides on the roundabout which attended the Show.

The Seaside (i) Great Yarmouth 1910

I well remember my first sight of the sea. I was eight years old. We children, all excited, went by train from Flordon to Yarmouth, our faces in turn glued to the train window till we arrived. A big shout went up as we spotted the sea. We just couldn't take it in at first, such a huge span of water. On the way to the beach, we were each bought a spade, for a penny, but only one bucket between us for fourpence. We were digging away almost before we reached the beach. What a day it was! We had rolls and cheese at midday, and a large glass of lemonade with ice cream in it, for fourpence. We were near a fair and had one ride each on the horses, for twopence each.

(ii) Gorleston 1910

I recall how excited we were (the four children in our family) when we went to Gorleston for our holiday in August, as it meant a journey by train. There were excursions from Norwich to Yarmouth for one and sixpence on Bank Holidays, but we never patronised these, as the long steam trains were crammed to bursting, and the passengers were often boisterous and the worse for drink.

Before the holiday came, the excitement of packing all the family's clothes into the large wicker dress basket sent luggage in advance, the overflow being stuffed into rush-hold-alls which we carried together with our spades and pails. We had a sitting room and bedrooms in the house of a landlady who let, who also prepared the food provided by mother.

We loved Gorleston, especially the jetty with the cosies below (anything but cosy to sit in!) and the sunny extension at the end. We could see the fishing boats come into the harbour and the 'Yarmouth Belle' packed with passengers from London. On the beach there was Punch and Judy and sometimes a pierrot show. Yarmouth, reached by a trip for sixpence in the river steamer, had more sophisticated pleasures, slot machines on Britannia Pier, and a photographer on the promenade who produced small dark photographs on a kind of tin backing.

(iii) Great Yarmouth 1920

It was some time before my sister and I were deemed mature enough to take a holiday by ourselves. The first adventure in this field was Great Yarmouth. We never thought the day complete without a dip in the briny. So, armed with our towels and voluminous bathing dress (which must perforce have a skirt) we hired a bathing hut. This was reminiscent of an old-type gipsy caravan. Horses were kept on the beach to draw these huts up and down according to the state of the tide. We mounted the steps on the landward side, locked the door and proceeded to unrobe. The door on the seaward side was straight down in to the water. By this door, a thick rope was attached and to this we clung as we gingerly crept down the steps into the water.

(iv) Great Yarmouth 1920

When we had measles it was a sorry day, but when we were later sent with my aunt to the sea for two weeks to recuperate it didn't seem so bad after all.
The beach services were part of our daily routine, when we and other children, led by the good man who organised these services, sang very lustily 'Oh to be a Little Sunbeam,' and many other hymns and songs.

Time off in Norwich (i) Street Carnivals 1924

In Norwich, each summer following the First World War, Carnivals were held in street groups or yards. The second Saturday in August 1924 the folk of Angel Yard had a carnival. I well remember the grown-ups dressed us up in fancy clothes. My big brother of four and a half years (one year my senior), was a bridegroom with top hat, tails and white shirt. Lily Barber from next door, was his bride, wearing a beautiful dress made from a white lace curtain, and she carried a big bunch of flowers.
I was dressed in a long pink garment with a blue sash, because I was a bridesmaid. I held on to a bunch of flowers, in a paper doily, and as the elastic in my knickers was loose, I held on to them as

well, only to be told time and time again: 'Mary, put your clothes down.'

(ii) The Steamboat Jenny Lind 1910

We enjoyed the trips down the river on the old steamboat *Jenny Lind*, to Bramerton Woods End with old Billy Bluelight, a well known local character, running along the bank catching pennies thrown to him. Once or twice, the boat took us the whole length of the Yare to Yarmouth Quay.

(iii) Whit Monday Parade of Horses 1910

Every year on Whit Monday there would be a parade of horses through the streets of Norwich, mostly Percherons and Shire horses beautifully groomed and decorated with ribbons.

Hospital Parades Aylsham 1910

The hospital parades are no more, alas! The people from villages for miles around came to town on those Sundays. All the Friendly Societies had their banners. On a windy day it took six men or youths to carry one. The men wore whitish trousers, green velvet coats and hats with feathers—the clothes I associated with Robin Hood's merry men.

Fairs (i) Southrepps 1880's

The lighter side of life in those days was the Village Fair held in June each year.
This was a very big affair and all sideshows were put up in the yards of the Public Houses and sometimes stretched down the main street.
The caravans were most attractive and the fair people were quite well known to villagers.
Children were given a holiday from school, Public Houses were always open and beer was twopence a pint.
During these two days horses and ponies were bought and sold, the

main street being used as a place to show off the paces of the animals.

(ii) Aylsham 1910

The twice yearly fairs, in March and September, with galloping horses, swings, coconut shies and glaring lights caused great excitement. We watched rock being 'pulled' at the back of the stall, and later could have purchased two lumps for a penny, had we not seen the lady spit on her hands!

(iii) Terrington St Clement 1930

One night there was a fair in the village. I was longing to see it at night, with the lights on the roundabouts, and to hear the especially noisy music. One of the maids put a ladder up to our bedroom window and down I climbed. This was after nine o'clock on a winter night and I had on my overcoat, with pyjama legs pulled up high underneath, so as not to show. I will never forget the excitement of that night's visit to the little fair. My elder sister, afraid to go herself, awaited my return, terrified that my parents might discover my absence. They didn't, and she was much relieved when I climbed back up that ladder, heard the maid and her 'follower' pull the ladder away, closed the window, and sat on the bed to eat the bar of nougat I had brought back. She was breathless at my daring.

(iv) Blakeney 1890's

Blakeney Regatta was a great day for the whole village and surrounding neighbourhood. The land sports were carried out on the Eyot, followed by the sailing races, rowing and sculling. There was the Ladies rowing race, with the Pages, Longs and Hudsons, all exhibiting their strength against each other. After the greasy pole and swimming races the great event of the day for many people was the Fair. For many years the Grays, Dacks, and Mrs Gizzi had visited Blakeney with their amusements and stalls. We were always pleased to see them each year and hope they, and their descendants, will always come.

(v) Blakeney 1920

I was a 'tweeny' in a doctor's house when Regatta day came with all the fun of the fair on the Quay. To my delight we were to be allowed out for the evening. We had to leave a buffet supper in the dining room. I was allowed to be out until ten o'clock, the others until eleven o'clock. By seven thirty we were ready to go. Cook said I was to stay up until they came in to make sure they were not locked out. I had a wonderful time with the garden boy. We each had five shillings to spend. Since swings and roundabouts were only twopence a ride, our money went a long way, and enjoying ourselves we forgot the time. When I did remember, I asked a man who I thought was the local 'bobby' what the time was. A strange policeman turned to me and started in a loud voice to sing: 'If you want to know the time ask a policeman.' I fled back to the house hoping I wouldn't be late. It was only five past ten and I breathed a sigh of relief and sat down to wait for the others. The doctor was working in the surgery and at eleven o'clock he came through, locked the door, and sent me to bed. From my attic window I could see the surgery light and I sat and waited for it to go out so that I could go down and unlock the door, but it began to dawn on me that the doctor intended to wait up until the others came in so I went to bed.

The next morning they told me they had come in through the coalhouse, which meant they had to get through a half-door, scramble over the coal and get to the door inside the house from which we filled the coal hods. But the doctor had the last word. He called them to the surgery and with a grin on his face said he wouldn't pay for their dresses to be laundered.

The Circus that cost too much Holt 1890

I do not regret my childhood days, in fact, they are very happy memories indeed. One is being taken to Holt, walking a distance of four miles to see a Circus go round the town. Not to *go* to the circus—that would have cost too much money.

Cherry Merry for Queen Victoria Burgh St Peter 1887

I remember Queen Victoria's Golden Jubilee, in 1887. What a day that was, with a meal of huge joints of beef, plum pudding and a substantial tea! After tea there were Sports. Fathers and Mothers all joined in 'Kissing in the Ring', and we finished up with fireworks. I am afraid a lot of men finished up a little 'cherry merry'.

Part Three

Religion and Society

Church and Chapel   Hard Times   The Social Ladder

Church and Chapel

One scarcely knows whether to sigh nostalgically for the orderliness of it all, the stability, the virtue, or to wonder how they could have suffered such boredom, or inflicted so many hours of sitting still in uncomfortable clothes on young things bursting with energy. But Chapel preachers seem to have had a sense of the dramatic to help to alleviate the boredom and the devil undoubtedly tempted with other interesting distractions.

The Strict Sunday Saxlingham 1890

When I was a child I used to be taken to Church three times on a Sunday: Matins in the morning, Sunday School in the afternoon and Evensong at night. We did not have many books in our home. The chief ones were the Bible and Pilgrims Progress, both well read. We were never allowed to knit or sew on Sundays nor even read a newspaper. Saturday night, the work basket, knitting and sewing, with the weekly newspaper folded on top were all put away in the cupboard till Monday.

Why We Sat So Still Strumpshaw 1920

Sunday School twice on Sundays come rain or shine and Morning Service till just before the sermon. No knitting or sewing on Sundays or toys—only one's best books. My! we sat still in Church, but who wouldn't with our petticoats and knickers starched stiff? Our hats had elastic bands to keep them on, and nasty boys would pull the elastic and then let go.

Hymns and Madam Butterfly Terrington St Clements 1930

On Sundays, after we had come home from Chapel and after our Sunday supper of cold beef and pickles, we often had musical evenings. We all played something and we all sang. We would gather round the baby grand piano and we would sing, and play hymns that we liked, and popular songs, like 'Wagon Wheels'. One sister played the violin, and my only brother the clarinet. We had everything in our repertoire, from nursery rhymes to Madam Butterfly and what we lacked in finesse we made up for in enthusiasm.

A Day's Rest for Men and Horses Foulsham 1920

I used to feel sorry for the horses at harvest time—they had to work so hard. How pleased they were when Saturday evening came and they were allowed to spend Sunday on the green meadows! No harvesting was ever done on my Father's farm on Sunday. In fact he was rather strict and we were not allowed to knit or sew, but only to read Sunday books.

Knicker Trouble Burgh St Peter 1890

We girls had to go to Church every Sunday. I shall never forget the experience I had one Sunday morning. Our long knickers used to button up behind, and as I rose to go up to the Communion rail the button came off. I had to hold them up as I went up to the chancel, and afterwards as I walked through the village. When the path led to a wood I hastily took off my drawers and stuffed them in my umbrella.

Segregation (i) Gimingham 1910

In those days the church and Rectory were enclosed by trees, now cut down, alas, and on the opposite side of the road were six magnificent beeches, known as the Grove. Under the largest of these the men of the village would congregate on Sunday mornings for an exchange of news before the bell rang for service. They did not of course accompany their wives to church but followed them in later, sitting on the two back seats close together whilst the women sat in twos and threes further up.

(ii) Near Wood Norton 1910

My husband remembers how, in a nearby church, the Rector's Brass Band used to play on Festival Days, seated in the west gallery. The Squire and farmers sat in the chancel, the working people in the nave, with the Sunday School children in front of them. These had been marched in from the Rectory where their lessons were held. Before the service began, the wives, mothers and younger women would be seated on the south side of the church, and as the five-minute bell began to toll the menfolk would straggle in and take their places on the north side. Families never sat together.

The Prodding Verger Mulbarton 1890

'I remember,' said the old man, as he looked at me from his bed, his eyes alight with memory, 'when I was a boy. That was nigh on eighty-five years ago. We lads were in the choir, and so was Dad. There was an old verger, and if we lads didn't behave ourselves, he'd prod us with a six-foot stick, which he kept for that purpose. Well! as I was a saying, one Sunday morning I started larking around. First he prodded me, and then seeing that that didn't stop me, he strode up, took me by the arm, and started marching me down the whole length of the aisle; and mind you, the Church was filled in them days. But I see'd the door open (it was summer you see) and I makes up my mind what I'd do. When we were opposite that door, I gave a good squirm and was off, and out of that Church before you could look around. Didn't I enjoy myself on the Common that morning! But when I got home me old Dad gave me such a hiding, and promised me worse if it should happen again.'

Distractions Runhall 1900

There was a chapel near our house. We went to Sunday School in the morning and to the Service in the afternoon. There was a small harmonium for the music. The ladies wore black coats and skirts and black bonnets tied under the chin with satin ribbon. Some of the bonnets had feathers or trimmings which waved about each time the head moved. This fascinated me so much, I forgot to listen to the sermon till the preacher thumped on the pulpit when he got excited.

There's the Devil! Wood Norton 1915

With the minor hardships of country life were also the delights of a country boyhood, ever remembered by my husband. In far-away France the first World War was raging, but on Sunday afternoons in the little chapel another war was fought out, far more alive and exciting to a small boy. The visiting preachers were passionate in their zeal against the Devil and their prayers would mount into a frenzy, spell-binding to themselves and their congregation. 'There's the Devil, Brother', cried one, roaring into the aisle. 'Howlld him Brother Daniel' shouted another, grabbing the first. The spell would break and each would return somewhat sheepishly to his seat; but it had been wonderful while it lasted, and quite unforgettable.

The Open-Air Service. Knapton 1890

Mother was a Methodist and we had to go to Chapel. I looked forward to the Camp meeting when the Preachers spoke from Wagons on a Meadow, and there was great singing and 'Amens' shouted from the Congregation.

Sunday Crime and Punishment Horningtoft 1890

I was born in 1885 in a small Norfolk village, the eldest of five boys, and two girls. My father was very particular in keeping the Sabbath day sacred, and all attending church once or twice on Sundays.
He would stand at the end of a seat and as we passed in, the youngest would sit next to him. One Sunday morning I walked on some thin ice over a ditch and slipped in over my knees and went home wet and muddy, was sent upstairs with a piece of food and given a verse of a hymn to learn during the afternoon. It was not a familiar hymn and I spent a miserable afternoon and wished I had not walked on the ice and had done as I was told.

The Musicians Gallery and Three-Decker Pulpit Southrepps 19th Century

My Mother, now aged ninety-seven, remembers her father telling her about the Parish Church.
In his day a gallery was always in use at the west end of the church. Besides seating some of the congregation it held men who provided music for the services, the instruments being, we think, fiddles. On the north side of the church was a three decker pulpit. In this the parish clerk would read a portion of the service at ground floor level, rising to platform two for more reading and finally the clergyman would preach the sermon from the upper platform.
All the pews were high box-like affairs and in the chancel, wooden benches provided seating for Sunday School children and choir.

The Organ Bellows Blower and his Mate Blakeney 1900

The centre-piece of our village is our beautiful church. One thing I remember from my childhood is seeing Mr Pitcher looking out of the doorway above the rood screen, as he was employed to sit up in the chamber above the chancel to blow the organ bellows. This was of course before electricity was installed, and a boy had to be employed to keep Mr Pitcher awake! The church was very cold, only being heated by oil lamps, and our Rector, who was elderly, often wore woollen gloves whilst taking the service.

The Early Ecumenical Spirit Swaffham 1920

The first house I remember living in was near the parish church. Our parents and grandparents were Primitive Methodists, so we were all sent to the Sunday School held at that chapel, until Mother found out that the Sunday School teacher was often late, and we were playing about the street. Great-Aunt Susan, who lived opposite the chapel saw this, so from then on we were sent to the parish church Sunday School, where Mother could see us nearly to the door. I used to think what a lovely church to go to. There were a lot more children, and we were allowed to take part in the service, pulling the bell or reading the lesson or taking up the collections. We had ten o'clock Sunday School service every Sunday and if we liked we could stay to the eleven o'clock service, which we often did as we used to like to see the boys come in from the Grammar School and various prominent people who were escorted by the churchwardens to their seats with their names in a little frame.

Flowers for the Sick and Elderly Sprowston 1910

Soon after the School Treat came the Annual Flower Service. On a given Sunday afternoon children brought posies of flowers to the church and during a special hymn walked in procession to the altar where a huge cross had been erected and all the flowers were laid on it, which made a marvellous colourful display. Afterwards the flowers were given to the sick and elderly people.

Hard Times

The 19th Century depression in farming which lasted well into this century laid a pall of crushing poverty over the agricultural workers of Norfolk. This we all know as a historical fact, and the injustice and harshness of it all, the great gap between rich and poor make us burn with retrospective indignation. Yet these writers who know what this poverty felt like express no bitterness. Were they too busy to think about the rights and wrongs? Was poverty in the country just that much more bearable than in the town? Was there some compensating factor that we have lost? There is probably no one valid explanation; but whilst admiring their stoicism, we must be glad that that sort of poverty has gone.

Them Days Rollesby 1900

It was a chance remark about wages which unlocked a store of memories about 'how we managed in them days'. They were told in a flow of purest Norfolk, with no expressions of self pity or resentment, only a sturdy pride in what they achieved on so very little, and I have written it down as exactly as I can remember.
'There were eleven on us, Mother, Father, and nine of us children. My sister May was the eldest, and I was the oldest boy, then came six more girls, and my brother Billy. We lived in Rollesby, in a house that ain't there now. My father was in the bullock shed all his working life, and worked for Mr Starling, Farmer. He earned fourteen shillings a week, and paid two shillings and sixpence rent. That included Sundays, of course, and he started at six in the morning. My mother had a lot to do at home, and could not earn anything, except a little fruit-picking, but in the autumn Mr Brownsword used to let her go on his meadow, and pick up acorns. Us children used to go and help her, and she got ninepence a bushel. We went to school, and we paid for our education in those days, and I took twopence. When I was eleven, there was some talk of getting five shillings a week for my parents, from the Parish. They came and asked questions, went into the matter, and the upshot of it was that I had to go out to work. I left school, and started work on a farm for four shillings weekly. So my parents never got the five shillings, they only got four.

My mother did a lot of cooking. She made up five stone of flour into bread every week, in two lots, three stone and two stone. One week when our oven had a hole in it, we had our bread off the baker, and we bought forty-two loaves. Mr Chapman, the butcher at Martham, was very good to us. On Saturday nights he would sell us a whole bag of scraps for one shilling, left over from his stall on Yarmouth market. My mother washed them well. Some of them bones had a lot of meat on, and we had stew with bread dumplings. She made twelve at a time, big as your head.

On Sundays we went to Sunday School. The children took a penny each week, and had a new pair of boots once a year. Every year my sisters all had a new dress from Mrs Brownsword at Rollesby Hall. My sister Elsie used to go up to the Hall Saturdays to do odd jobs. One thing she used to do was lead the pony that pumped the water out of the well. The pony went round and round in a circle, attached to a long shaft. My sister used to drive the pony to Martham Station to fetch parcels, too.

My grandmother sent me some bantams, two hens and a cock. After that I always had bantams and eggs. One day when I came home from work, I found that my father had sold some of my bantams to buy a pair of working boots. I can tell you, I *was* done, but I suppose things were hard for him too. I used to feed a neighbour's rabbits for him, and he gave me one young one out of each litter. I earned money by running errands, shopping, kindling, and helping on the farm, and I was never without a little money of my own. Even before I left school I gave my Mother one shilling a week for my clothes. Seven shillings and sixpence bought a pair of working boots, and we were glad of left-offs of clothing.

All on us are still alive and working. The oldest is seventy-five, so we ain't got a lot to grumble about, have we?'

Wages (i) Farmworkers Burgh St Peter 1880

In those days farm workers earned ten shillings a week, and worked from six o'clock in the morning until six o'clock at night. They were up at four o'clock Harvest Time, mowing the barley while the dew was on. (Now they wait until four o'clock in the afternoon for the dew to go off.)

(ii) Harvest Price Drayton 1912

The men worked long hours. They got so much for the harvest. I remember once it was eight pounds. They tried to get it done quickly as many relied on this money for their rent or for their children's clothes, etc. If the weather was wet and they couldn't get on, it was quite a calamity.

(iii) Gardener to a Gentleman Drayton 1912

When I was seven we moved to Drayton. I lived with my grand-parents. My grandfather was gardener to a gentleman who lived there while he was having a house built near North Walsham. I remember my granny being excited because he was to get one pound a week when he came to work here.

(iv) In Service Halesworth 1894

When I was 14 I went into service. I worked for eighteenpence a week, that was eighteen shillings and sixpence a quarter. When I took my first quarter's wages, my mistress said to me: 'If you save ten shillings, I will give you another ten shillings, and I will take you to Halesworth to put it in the Post Office.' I did, and I have never been without a pound from that day to this.

Soup for the Poor Mulbarton 1890

'Every Tuesday and Thursday when I was a boy,' said the old man, 'me and my Sister would take the milk boiler and go down to the Rectory—five o'clock prompt. We'd go into the kitchen and there was the "copper" copper. It really *was* copper, steaming full of hot soup—oh boy! the smell—it was good! There was the parson standing with a list and calling out "Mrs X three pints". The server would then dole out the three pints for the said Mrs X. We always had four pints, and you can be sure we always had a sup or two before we got home. Though to be sure we'd always say "No" if our Mother asked us if we'd been drinking it. For tea we'd all be given a bowl of hot soup and a thick hunk of bread. I remember the smell and the taste of that soup to this day.'

One Man's Life Knapton 1882-1970

My father is now eighty-eight. This is what he remembers of his life:— 'Knapton is a small village where I was born in 1882. To Thomas and Eliza Bane. There were eight of us children.

Father was a Farm Worker and earned ten shillings a week. Times were hard. Mother used to take in washing from gentry in Mundesley and North Walsham. She would fetch it in the Old Chap's dicky and cart—that's how she found out he went in pubs as the dicky stopped at the ones he used.

I well remember going to Knapton Hall for soup they made for the poor of the Parish. Old Grimes lived there then. We'd take the biggest boiler we could find. Many a time we had to share an egg and a herring between two.

The gipsies used to camp up Green Lane. I'd be up there like a shot as I always had a good feed with them. I tasted hedgehog they'd caught, rolled in wet clay, and baked. When it was cooked the whole skin came off as clean as a whistle. One Arm Waterfield (his wife had one eye!) was the best of the gipsies. The caravans were spotless and the brass all shining.

I left school when I was twelve, and my first job was at Church Farm. Pains farmed it then. I was paid one shilling a week for cleaning shoes, knives and forks and milking the cows and cleaning out stables. I had my first pipe of baccy there in the stable, blowing the smoke out of the pop hole but I got caught and got a hiding off my Old Chap, but that didn't stop me, when I could get hold of some. It couldn't have cost much as Mother took most of my money. I soon left there and went to Johna Walpole's at Edingthorpe and got five shillings for a seven day week feeding bullocks. Soon I bought my first dicky off Waterfield. At that time the railway was being built from North Walsham to Mundesley. The only time I left Knapton was to work at Felixstowe on the sea front from Cobbles Wall to the Fletchers Public House.

It was hard work barrowing shingle from the beach. When I came back I helped to make the road from Mundesley to Trimingham. Breaking stones with a hammer. After that I went back to bullock feeding. On Market Day we had to drive the cattle from Norwich calling at different farms on the way, sometimes leaving them somewhere for the night and carrying on next day. After I married I lived and worked at Bacton. Poaching was my pastime then, I had a good dog called Fly. She let me know if the bobby or gamekeeper was about. Sometimes some of my mates would go, then we'd net rabbits—and don't tell me there isn't ghosts, as I saw one near Bacton Church one moonlight night.
As we didn't have much money to spend, we had to find our own amusements. On Guy Fawkes Night we had a spree.
The General Strike was a bad time. My brother Tom went to America and sister Eliza to Canada. They are still alive and well.
As I said before, times were hard but the food we had was good and pure.
I never thought I would live to see men walking on the moon, but I'm glad to be alive and well to tell the tale.'

Half an Egg for Breakfast Drayton 1912

My cousin used often to come to stay. We used to share everything. He and I used to have half an egg for breakfast or half a kipper cut lengthwise and we never forgot whose turn it was to have the fat side. How we enjoyed the homemade bread my Granny made! We didn't have as much to choose from as the children of today. They have so much offered them they don't know what they want, I sometimes think.

The Lost Sixpence Matlaske 1910

One holiday morning I was walking along the village street when I saw a mobbing woman and a bla'ring boy searching in the dust. 'Oh Miss he's been a shop for me and he's lorst his sixpence change—lorst his sixpence change he has.' She wailed more loudly and the boy bla'red louder still. Suddenly there was the coin by my toe. I shouted my find, and the mother ran calling blessings on me. 'Oh Miss. I hope you will never know what sixpence means to me.' Wages were very low then and families were large.

The Poor Widows Southrepps 1880

My mother, now aged ninety-seven, remembers that in the early 1880s a crude form of public assistance was carried on in a shed in the yard of the present butchers shop.
Very poor widows gathered there each week to receive one and sixpence in money and a small quantity of flour.
Sometimes a long wait in the wintry weather would have to be endured as the relieving officer (as he was known) came in a pony cart from Beckham. The poor old ladies all wore shawls.

The Kinship of Poverty Sandringham 1920

One old Norfolk man I knew could tell the time on sunny days by putting up a stick and watching the shadow. Few could afford a watch. This poverty, shared by most, made for a sharing of joys and sorrows, and a feeling of kinship that is lost today. The daily lives of these old men and women are my finest memories.

The Social Ladder

Some were content to accept the gap between the lower and the upper rungs as part of the natural order of things, and 'bopping' to one's elders and betters was just part of this natural order. But for those with ambition, there were many different ways of closing the gap, including having drawers with lace on, a piano in the front room, a lavatory with a chain, and maids to wait at table.

Benevolent Royalty Sandringham 1920

I have childhood memories of Sunday School at West Newton and of walking in all weathers across the park to Sandringham for morning service, and sitting in a small alcove with the tattered colours of the Norfolks, hanging overhead, and seeing all the heads of state who came with the Royal Family. As a child I went with my school to take a wreath when Queen Alexandra died. She was not only a Queen to us but someone who, with Princess Victoria, visited our day school, gave us presents at Christmas and took an interest in our wellbeing.

Benevolent Squire Swanton Novers 1900

At Christmas we went to the big house in the park and there, in the huge Servants' Hall we had a sumptuous tea and we were each given, for the girls, a length of dress material, and for the boys, shirt material.

The Accepted Order Hardingham 1890

We had a school master and mistress, whom we all loved and respected. When we saw them in the village, we made them a curtsy and the boys touched their caps, as we did to all the gentry.

The Newcomers (i) Aylsham 1910

My kind, loving mother, years ahead of her time, dressed her little girls in summer in short gay cotton frocks with matching 'pants' and no petticoats. We knew the freedom of bare legs and soft plimsolls.

The Vicar's wife came to protest at this lack of modesty. As comparative newcomers we did not know that it was the custom for girls to curtsy and boys to touch their caps when they met her—but they were excellent Vicarage folk. Later, hearing that we liked reading, she gave us the run of her nursery library.

(ii) Drayton 1912

My granny always said it was the proper way to start the week to go to church. The clergy mixed with the people then and took an interest in their families. We had some true friends among them. They were ready to help and advise in time of trouble. The one at Drayton was a Canon—I can't remember his name—he was rather a pompous man. The first time I went to Drayton village by myself I met him and he held up his walking stick and said: 'Nod your head, nod your head'. I looked at him in amazement. I learned afterwards it was the correct thing to do. He visited the school sometimes. Children were more respectful and well behaved to their elders then. There was such a difference between rich and poor then.

(iii) Matlaske 1910

When parson or squire came by the boys pulled the forelock and girls bopped. My father was the schoolmaster, and following parental instruction I said: 'Good morning Sir'. The girls said in awe 'You never bopped', expecting clouds of wrath to descend on my stiff-kneed irreverence.

The Social Hierarchy Matlaske 1910

The son of the local ratcatcher considered himself to be a step above the other boys whose fathers were ploughmen or cowmen or shepherds or teamsters. In local language, he was 'botty' and was nicknamed 'Bot Thaxter'. I often had to stay in at playtime because my father, the schoolmaster, was strict with me. One morning Bot, who sat behind me, had written his composition on his slate and signed it with his full name. I rubbed it out with my slate rag and I wrote BOT. He dared not pay me out because public opinion was not on the side of the botty boy.

Social Longings (i) Shipdham 1917

We wore jerseys, pleated kilts and bloomers for school. Some little girls wore drawers with lace on and white starched pinafores. I thought this the last word in elegance, but vanity wasn't encouraged in our house and bloomers were my lot. When I stood in class and recited: 'And to do my duty in that state of life unto which it may please God to call me,' I mentally added: 'But *please* give me fat legs' (which were thin), 'and drawers with lace on.'

(ii) Drayton 1912

Some of the girls at school who lived in houses with bay windows and had a piano in the front room I thought were the elite.

Moving Up in the Town Norwich 1920

We lived in Angel Yard in Norwich. One day, the postman gave me a letter to give to my Dad. We were all eager to know what was in that long white envelope, as we didn't often receive many like that. It was put on the mantel shelf to be opened by Dad when he came home from the shoe factory where he worked, and what excitement that caused. He turned to my Mother and said: 'Well, we have one at last'. Then everyone started talking at once, and there was lots of laughing. Mother went next door to let them know we 'had one'. Then I heard that we were going to move into a nice new Council house. After a lot of talking and packing, Dad came home with a huge hand cart. On it he stacked chairs, tables, beds, oddments, in fact, after two or three trips our little house was empty.

At last all the odds and ends were packed onto the last cart load. Soot the cat, was put into a straw basket my Dad used when he went fishing. Baby and Margy were put into the pram, with all the blankets and sheets, and I was lifted onto the cart holding the basket with the cat in.

My Dad, who was a hard working man, with dark curly hair and hazel eyes, sang as he pushed his heavy load, my mother smiling as always, pushed the big heavy pram and its contents.

When we arrived at our new home, my Dad lifted me down from the cart, and as I stretched my stiff legs, I looked at the great big house in front of me. It seemed huge compared to the one we had just left. It had five large windows and a door at the front, and more windows and a door at the back.

As I walked through the front door I saw in front of me a huge stairway with beautiful red shining lino, which was held in place with steel rods all shining like silver. Oh! We were rich!

And all the rooms looked huge and seemed quite empty with the furniture from our little old house. While I was exploring the small rooms and cupboards, I found the lavatory. It was such a dear little room with a huge white basin that had a brown wooden seat that lifted up. Over the top of the funny basin was the tank. A chain with a handle hanging down got my little brain working. I discovered that if the chain was pulled down, lots of water swished around the inside of the huge white basin, then disappeared out of sight.

I spent many a time just pulling that chain.

Moving Up in the Country Terrington St Clement 1930

Then our beautiful new house was built for us. I remember watching the walls go up and up, and finally moving in and the excitement of having hot water out of gleaming taps and bathing in what seemed to be our enormous white bath. Wonderful indeed after bathing in our old galvanised bath in front of the kitchen fire.

And this was the era of maids. Everyone seemed to boast, or complain of the maids.

I remember the girls at school judging each other's wealth by the number of maids each had. And sometimes, I suspect, inventing an extra one to impress their friends. We had two. And how well I remember our family sitting round a very large dining table, Mother at one end, and Father at the other, and Mother slapping her palm on the little bell, to ring for the food to be brought in.

Part Four

Work and Wheels

The Farming World   Other Crafts and Trades   School   Getting about

The Farming World

Country people's memories revolve of course around farming, the basic and the oldest industry of all; and for centuries the memories of seedtime and harvest have not differed fundamentally from generation to generation.
But the memories recorded here of the period of change from the traditional ways of pre-mechanical age farming to fully mechanised farming have a special significance. A mere half-century has rubbed out from first-hand experience all the centuries that have gone before and soon no one will remember the old ways.

When the horse was king (i) Blakeney 1890

At the Manor House, in my childhood, we made our own amusements in and around the garden and farm-yard, watching the hay-cutter which was worked by a horse fixed to a shaft, which it turned very slowly, a man sitting in a seat at the centre. Our delight was to sit on the shaft and have rides. There was also sheep-shearing to watch, and a visit from the harness-makers from Holt, when long trestle tables would be set out in the top barn.
For a week the men would work at the overhauling of the harness for all the horses, approximately forty with cart and riding-stable horses.

(ii) Foulsham 1920

Gone now are the teams of horses from the farms but how fond the teamsmen were of their charges! They had to arrive at work about five o'clock in the mornings to feed the horses before they commenced their day's work at seven. I used to feel sorry for the horses during the harvest when they had to cut the corn with the sail cutter and later the binder. They used to get so hot walking round and round the fields. The teams were generally changed halfway through the day to give them a rest.
At harvest time we children always used to take tea or 'fourses' as it was called, into the field. We loved to ride in the empty waggons, or on the horses' backs and sometimes we had to drive the pony

who had to walk round and round keeping the elevator working when the corn was being stacked.

(iii) Sandringham 1920

My brother from an early age drove the elevator horse. He sat in a little box and the horse went round and round all day turning the elevator shaft.

(iv) Griston 1920

As we had a foal or two each year from the working mares, the stallion arrived periodically, led by a man who either walked with him, or drove a horse and cart. Haymaking and harvest caused much excitement among the youngsters. Horse-drawn mowers and binders were in use. After turning the hay, all hands turned out to put it in cocks, where it stayed until fit to cart. When the corn was cut, numerous boys turned up to run down the rabbits which bolted out as the binder approached. Then the sheaves of corn were shocked up, a few being put aside to take to the Church for decorating purposes for the Harvest Thanksgiving. Finally the carting and stacking, with one team of workers in the field and another at the stack, and a hold-yer boy driving the loads.

(v) Neatishead 1930

The use of horses meant work for the tradesmen of the village. I well remember two blacksmiths, one wheelwright and two collar-makers in the village. These businesses have now gone; in the place of one is a petrol filling station and small garage.

Mechanical Progress (i) Saxlingham 1890

I remember the first sail cutter going into the field to cut the corn. Before that the corn was scythed. Men used to go into the field and cut a way for the cutter. The cutter drawn by two horses cut the corn; the men followed, tied it into sheaves, and stood it up in shocks all over the field to dry out before it could be carted and stacked. When the self-binder arrived there was tremendous excitement. The villagers all went along into the field to see this wonderful machine that cut and tied the corn. It was a great wonder.

(ii) Griston 1930

All the land work in those days was done by horses until a tractor arrived called an 'Overtime'. Once we had the land deep ploughed by a plough pulled through the land by traction engines stationed opposite each other, either side of the field. Threshing was a great excitement. Special steam coal had to be ordered. The engine and drum arrived the evening before the appointed day and manoeuvred into place. Next morning the engine driver arrived in advance to stoke up and raise the steam, then everyone to their appointed places and threshing commenced. By the end of the day, everyone looked pretty black as it was a dusty job, especially for the man who looked after the chaff and caulder. Rats were dealt with by the farm terrier and anybody who happened to hold a stick or broach as the sticks were called which held the thatch in place on top of the stack. In those days a windmill in the next village was still used to grind corn. When a new sail was required, I remember seeing many willing helpers heaving it up from the ground with ropes.

The Lord of the Harvest Sandringham 1910

In those days there were strict rules of harvest procedure. Each man had a written set of rules though many could not read them. The Lord started first, finished first, settled all disputes, and negotiated with the farmer on all matters. This was so with the hoeing of root crops. My father was Lord for many years; I can remember how cross he used to be when the weather was wet and no money was earned.

The Harvest Frolic Shotesham 1900

I loved to watch the men mowing the barley. It must have been very hard work, but it was a lovely sight and sound. I can hear the swish of the scythes now. We used to have rides in the empty waggons. When the last of the corn was stacked, we would have what they called in those days, a Harvest Frolic. One of the barns would be decorated with leaves and berries. Cakes, puddings and huge joints of meat would be cooked by some of the women. In the evening, the men and their wives and also the children would sit down to a lovely supper and there would be beer for the men and some of them would get quite merry and there would be a sing song.

I remember one old chap in particular singing: 'I've got sixpence, a jolly, jolly sixpence, I love sixpence better than my life.' He sang this song every year; I think it must have been the only one he knew.

Gleaning Shotesham 1900

After harvest was finished we went gleaning and would get quite a lot for the pigs and chickens. We would have aprons with large pockets in the front to put the short ears in and those with long straws would be tied into bunches.

The Season's Round Mulbarton 1900

'I remember'—magic words for a seventy-year-old with so many memories of her beloved Norfolk—of a peaceful slow-moving age when time was measured by the seasons' round of ploughing, seed-time and harvest; memories of the first lambs, the first primroses on banks sheltered by high hedges, hot days in the harvest fields, biting winter winds, and over all the wide, ever changing skies.

One of my earliest recollections is of grandfather's farm at Mulbarton at the beginning of the century. All work was done by hand, milking, broadcasting seed, reaping with sickles and stacking, while horses helped with ploughing, harrowing and carting. The great event of the year was the harvest. Men worked while daylight lasted, then by the light of the moon, wives bringing their meals, 'elevenses' and 'fourses' to the fields. When the last load was carted the labourers were paid an agreed sum for the harvest. One year I remember it was ten pounds. Then came the harvest home in the big barn, an abundant feast prepared by grandmother and aunts, followed by an evening of singing and dancing. The harvest money was spent in Norwich on clothes for the coming winter.

The skim milk was sold to the labourers for a halfpenny a pint. Corn was taken to the mill for grinding, and the huge sails and roaring machinery fascinated me, as did too the fiercely burning fire and flying sparks as the blacksmith fashioned shoes for the horses.

The Farm by the Sea Waxham 1900

Waxham, where our farm was, was a really rural village at that time—no school, no shop, no pub. All our corn and farm produce went by wherry to Yarmouth where it was ground and came back as flour and meal for the cattle; also our coal came from Yarmouth the same way.

In November 1900 we had a terrible storm and a shipwreck in our 'Gap'. I can remember the lifeboat coming from Palling drawn by six farm horses and our farm horses taking it back. Our kitchen was a casualty station. Two of the crew were saved and three died in the wreck—it was a Swedish ship. Luckily our kitchen range was always going and in the afternoon my father drove the two saved men wrapped up in blankets to the Seamans Home in Yarmouth.

The Dairy (i) Butter for the market Attleborough 1910

The dairy adjoined the kitchen where the separator was in daily use, separating the cream from the milk by two spouts at right angles.

In those days, this was a hand process and the handle of the machine had to be turned very evenly and continued by the next person who took over the rhythm without any deviation in this long and tedious operation.

Next was the butter making, when the cream was put into a large wooden churn. This also had to be hand turned continuously until one heard the 'plop, plop' of the butter forming. Then the bung on one side of the barrel was opened for the butter milk to drain away after which the large lid-like door on the opposite side was opened for the butter to come out.

After being slightly salted, it was shaped with wooden butter pats into one pounds and half pounds. Then a wooden wheel with a flower pattern was rolled across each pat, and it was wonderful to see this decoration appear on the butter.

The pats were then laid on greaseproof paper in a large basket, like a butcher's basket, covered with a white linen cloth, and put into the back of the dogcart with other baskets of eggs, sacks of corn, and other produce ready for the market. Sometimes, if there was room, we children had a ride to Attleborough where the produce was sold.

(ii) Bartering the butter Foulsham 1920

The other day we had a hymn in the Sunday Morning Service which brought memories of my childhood to me. It was 'Lead Kindly Light' which my father often sang as he turned the separator in the dairy. This machine skimmed the cream from the milk. The cream was kept in large earthenware creampots for about a week and then made into butter. My mother used to take some of this to the village shop about a mile away. She walked, carrying the half-pounds of butter in a hamper type basket which had been made by the local village basket maker, who incidentally made me a doll's cradle. The butter was exchanged for groceries and I can see the shopkeeper now as she weighed the sugar into the blue sugar bags.

Pin-money for the farmer's wife Foulsham 1920

My mother always reared turkeys for her pin-money. In those days they needed endless attention. Hard boiled eggs and nettles cut up finely were their staple diet for the first weeks. Very often they contracted diseases and there were no antibiotics to cure them. Blackhead was a horrible complaint. The ones that did survive and grew large were allowed to roam the stubble after harvest and pick up the corn which had been shed out. They were very fond of acorns too. When Christmas drew nearer they were brought home and shut up in a pen to fatten.

Droving (i) Sheep Great Moulton 1920

My village is fourteen miles from Norwich and it was not at all unusual to walk there when my father was young. He often tells of starting off at six in the morning to drive a flock of sheep to Norwich market. It was a tiring trip, as the sheep found a hundred and one diversions on the way. It was a very weary and footsore lad who accepted the arranged lift home in a horse-drawn cart at about two in the afternoon, and he didn't have to count sheep that night to get to sleep.

(ii) Geese Old Catton 1900

Many years ago my father worked for a man in Old Catton as groom and gardener, and among his many duties he had to help with driving hundreds of geese from Thorpe Station, Norwich; they had been brought from Holland. After having their wings clipped they would be driven through the streets of Norwich, just as the cattle were driven. They would drive them up Prince of Wales Road, Tombland and Magdalen Street to meadows to be fattened-up for Christmas. The women relatives of the workmen plucked these geese in time for the Christmas trade in a huge barn for threepence each goose. To make no mistake of the numbers plucked, they pulled the tongue out of each goose and would be paid threepence for each tongue.

(iii) Cattle Matlaske 1910

Summer Sunday mornings we would wake to the lowing of cattle being driven home from Norwich market, the drover walking all the way through the night.

Furriners on the Farm (i) Germans Attleborough 1916

Our farm holidays continued during the First World War when German prisoners were used to clear the ditches and rivers. One party came to the farm, as we had a small river running between the meadows. These Germans didn't work very hard and seemed happy. We used to go and see them each day with the watchful eye of Aunt Susan looking from the farm windows to see we came to no harm. The prisoners made us toys from wood in the hedges and we in turn took them bags of sweets (my father seemed to get a supply from somewhere). The British soldiers on guard told us we mustn't bring sweets, which to us children seemed unkind (not knowing what a prisoner was really).

The food the Germans had whilst working was a kind of broth, I think, heated in a huge cauldron over a wood fire in the field. One prisoner, an officer (a confectioner in Berlin in civilian life), when he came up to the farm for a supply of water asked to see Aunt Susan's oven in the wall. He also asked for eggs and the daily papers, speaking perfect English. These he would sit and read on the grass before returning to the meadow with a guard always with a fixed bayonet. The eggs, the German would quietly drop into the broth and when cooked take them out and eat them behind some bushes.

Their navy uniform had large red patches somewhere very visible. I remember asking why and was told: 'So that they could be easily seen if trying to escape'.

(ii) Dutchmen Aylsham 1914

One year there was the thrill of hearing a strange foreign language on the farm, particularly when the Dutchmen held a sing-song in the evenings. This was when they came to teach the Norfolk farmers how to grow and harvest sugar beet. They insisted on certain methods, such as using a two-tined fork, and then handling the beet by hand.

When the war broke out and they were still over here, I can remember local people regarding these 'Furriners' as possible spies.

Other Crafts and Trades

It is easy to feel sentimental about the lost world of independent, self-employed craftsmen in a world of mass production and huge factories. The existence of these craftsmen must certainly have made the village and small town a more closely-knit community, and village boys could grow up with first-hand knowledge of many crafts from which to choose their own. But all did not become craftsmen, and there were many soul and body destroying jobs before the days of mass production.

For village girls the choice of work outside the home was practically limited to 'going into service'—which in many cases meant 'going into servitude'. But fortunately not always; some became valued family friends and benevolent rulers of the households they served.

In Service (i) The Lowest Form of Humanity Swanton Novers 1917

At the age of fifteen I left home for a big house about thirty miles away, to take my place as third housemaid in a staff of twelve (almost the lowest form of humanity) for a salary of twelve pounds a year.

(ii) The Tweeny Blakeney 1920

About fifty years ago in Norfolk, all that girls leaving the village school could do was to go into domestic service, more often than not starting as a between maid in a local household, maybe the Hall, the Manor, the Rectory or the doctor's.

This was to be the way that I was to start work. School broke for the summer holidays on Thursday, 28th July. I was fourteen on the Friday. No holiday for me. We went straight from childhood to adults in those days. I was to start work on my fourteenth birthday at the doctor's house.

For weeks I had been seaming and felling after school hours helping my mother make my uniform which consisted of two print dresses, six morning aprons, four caps, four afternoon aprons, two blue check aprons, one hessian apron for scrubbing and a black alpaca afternoon dress. My wages were to be one pound a month which had to be taken home to help pay for my outfit.

Looking back I think what a pathetic little figure I must have looked going to my first place. Long coat, hair pinned up in a bun, with my brown paper parcel under my arm containing my uniform. I arrived at the house at three o'clock and without more ado was told to change into uniform and was then given my first task. This was to prepare the nursery tea. A heavy black tray with food, drink and crockery for Nannie and two children to be carried up the backstairs and along a landing. Laying the table under the eagle eye of Nannie was a bit nerve-racking. I felt she was waiting to pounce on my slightest mistake.

Kitchen tea came next which meant half an hour's break. At six o'clock we started to prepare dinner. I had to prepare vegetables and be general dogsbody to the cook until twenty past seven when it was 'wash your hands, change your apron, straighten your cap and help the parlour maid in the dining-room'. My dislike of parlour work started from that moment. To me it seemed ridiculous for two maids to wait on four people who could easily help themselves.

Dinner over, washing up done there were beds to be turned down, candlesticks and matches to be left in the front hall. In the kitchen oatmeal had to be brought to the boil and put in the hay box overnight. Supper came next consisting of bread and cheese and cocoa unless there were leftovers from the dining room which couldn't be kept till next day. At ten o'clock we went to bed, I wishing myself back home.

Up at six o'clock next morning to light the kitchen range which had to be blackleaded and polished till it shone. The plates to be cleaned with emery paper.

Then there were the surgery floors to be scrubbed, three large door-steps to be hearthstoned winter and summer. One task I loved in summer but hated in winter was to go along the front drive and clean the doctor's brass plate.

Morning tea had to be taken upstairs at a quarter to eight. Breakfast for the kitchen was at eight o'clock, for the dining room and nursery at eight thirty. Again that heavy tray to be taken upstairs. After breakfast I had to help the house maid until noon, then help cook prepare lunch and afterwards wash up and clean the kitchen floor. The rest of the afternoon was taken up helping the parlour-maid clean brass and silver. Tea-time again and so ended my first twenty-four hours as a tweeny.

As time went by I found there was a lighter side to service. Although I had known the garden boy at school as a friend of my brother's I began to see him in a new light. Maybe a little fellow feeling because we both received the rough end of everybody's tongue. But we had many a laugh together if I was sent into the garden to fetch anything he had forgotten to bring in, and cups of tea together on cook's day off.

Our time off was one afternoon and evening a week, every other Sunday afternoon and evening. The alternate Sunday we were allowed to go to morning service. But if we had visitors to lunch it often meant our time off started about four o'clock. Since I had to be in by nine o'clock it was a short half-day.

All spare china, and there was plenty of it, was kept in a cupboard on the landing and at spring cleaning time it all had to be brought downstairs to be washed. When the china was all put back, the mistress being out or so we thought, we decided to have a bit of fun and ride downstairs on the trays. I went first and just as I landed at the bottom, the mistress came round the hall. I picked up my tray and fled to the kitchen, leaving the others to face the music.

I was feeling a bit rebellious one morning when the mistress said: 'Child you've left a cobweb in the bathroom, you never look above your nose'. I answered back pertly, 'I must look above my nose, my eyes are above it'. This was reported to mother as being very rude and when I went home my mother gave me this advice: 'If you feel justified in answering back start by saying "excuse my seeming rudeness", then you can say what you have to.'

It always seemed a mystery to me how so many pennies could get under the edges of carpets, but Dad knew the answer. He said it was either a test of my honesty or to see if I swept under the edges. He told the mistress that I was to pocket any pennies I found among the dirt. I never found another one.

My dislike of parlour work grew and the last straw came one evening when there was a dinner party for the son home from flying school. While I was holding out the vegetables he pulled at my apron strings. He grabbed so hard that the button came off my skirt; feeling it slipping off, I put the vegetable dishes on the table and fled to the kitchen. This is the end, I thought, I will not wait at table any more.

My next halfday I went home and told my mother I was leaving. She said I must stay for a year to get a reference. So I had to go back, but on my fifteenth birthday I gave a month's notice. It was a month of sheer hard work, but the thought of escaping that dining room work kept me going and during that month I found myself a place as scullerymaid in the household of Lord and Lady Glamis where I could stay in the kitchen and learn to cook.

(iii) A Room to Herself Sprowston 1920

Agnes was the maid. I adored her. She came from Wroxham and her sisters were in service too. A special treat was for me to be allowed to stay in the kitchen with her and have my lunch and not go into the dining room with mother. When she had finished washing up she would take a large brown can filled with hot water from the copper in the scullery and take me up to her room where she changed into black frock and white cap and apron for the afternoon. She always seemed so proud of *her* room. I suppose it was the first time she had had a room to herself. She would put the water into a large flowered bowl on the marble-topped washing stand and I would stand on a chair and wash her back. Mother never did find me there.

(iv) On the receiving end of service Griston 1920

There always seemed to be more time in those days, and of course, more people to do the work.

Our household ran very smoothly, as the chief helper was old Ellen whose word was law. She arrived when my father was a boy and stayed with our family for forty years. I was very fond of her, and although she would stand no nonsense, she often spoilt me by making special dishes which she knew I liked. Ellen was of ample proportions, and as she got near retiring age, had difficulty in getting about quickly, owing to her 'rheumatics', brought on, she thought, by getting wet in her childhood, as she left school very early and had to go to work crow scaring in the fields.

Ellen's official work was the cooking, which included baking bread in the wall oven, once or twice a week. The everyday cooking was done on an Eagle kitchen range, which had to be lit every morning, with flue cleaning and black leading once a week.

As we had a farm, butter was made every week. Ellen made the butter into pounds and half-pounds and taught me how to make fancy pats and bird's nests.

As well as these duties she waited on my grandmother who lived with us, and also did odd sewing jobs and made gollywogs for various children. Once a year she took the day off and went in the donkey-cart to see a friend in a neighbouring village.

Besides Ellen, we had a house-maid, or rather a succession of them, always called Emma by my grandmother, whatever their real name. Also, a woman who came in to do the washing once a week. She stayed to dinner in the kitchen as the process lasted all day, commencing with the lighting of two coppers, one for hot water and one for boiling the whites.

The Teamsman Shotesham 1900

Sometimes my father would have to go to Blofield with sacks of corn and two of us children would be allowed to go with him if it was during the school holidays. This didn't happen very often and we had to take turns. I was thrilled when it was my turn. My mother would get us up early and pack sandwiches and shortcakes for us. We had to be up early and walk to the farm, where my father would be ready to start.

He would lift us up and we sat on the sacks of corn and we had a lovely view of the countryside. As we neared Stoke we could see Norwich Cathedral and Castle in the distance.

It would be midday before we arrived at Blofield. My father would stop at the King's Head public house where there would be another man who had come from Maltby with an empty waggon. Mr Fellowes, his employer, had a farm there.

They would feed their horses and rest them and would have a drink and a mardle together. He would buy us a ginger pop and my sister and I would go down a country lane and have a picnic. After the horses had had about two hours' rest we would make the return journey, this time in the empty waggon but the same horses. They were lovely creatures and my father was very kind to them; they knew his every word.

I can remember one time my father falling asleep as we were going through Trowse on the way home. A policeman shouted at him and woke him up telling him to look after his horses. 'They will be alright' he answered, 'they know their way home', and they did. I am not surprised he went to sleep, he had to be up very early in the morning and worked late: and as he was a teamsman, he had to look after his horses on Sunday.

Village Craftsmen Shipdham 1920

I remember the blacksmith and the smell of burning horses' hooves; the harness maker with an array of horses' collars standing outside the shop in the sun; the carrier's cart that went to the nearest market town and the mail cart that took our letters twenty miles to the nearest postal town and returned with letters for delivery early the following morning. There was the scavenger who plied his trade on moonlight nights, the grave digger who complained when business was bad, and the mole catcher.

A Prosperous Little Village Reedham 1910

I was born at Reedham in the year 1906. At that time Reedham was a prosperous little village. Along the riverside stood the old flint built Malt-house. The barley was brought in by horse and tumbril and wherry; it was soaked and roasted and taken to the nearby breweries the same way. This same old Malt-house is used today for a firm of boat builders, but today the boats are made of fibreglass, not timber.

The foundry stood on the hill and not very far from the school, indeed, near enough for us children to run that far at play time to watch the horses from the farm being shod.

Little Willie Hindle owned the foundry, and as well as being a very clever craftsman where ironwork was concerned, was also organist at the Church.
We often made trips to the foundry for Willie Hindle would make my granny's heaters for the box-iron. As a special favour he would make them with a hole through so they could be easily hooked out of the fire and slipped into the box.
The Flour Mill which stood in Mill Road was burnt down in about 1912, but I well remember going there for flour, with a clean pillow case.
About once a fortnight the Sale Yard near the Station was a very busy place. The cattle all came by road in those days, sometimes crossing the river on the old ferry boat; a few came by rail. The shouting of the drovers, the blaring of the cattle, plus some that got a bit out of hand, used to conjure up in our childish imagination scenes of wild bulls and greatly to be feared. Village life in those days was very pleasant. Everyone knew what was going on in the village; we had two elderly midwives and our own undertaker, so the news of births and deaths was soon known.
Wales' timber yard was situated along the river side and the trees were sawn there to provide timber for the boatyard. The boatyard, where the Norfolk wherries were built, provided work for most of the village, I suppose. It was called Hall's boatyard and was regarded as the best, and many wherries were built by my grandfather, some of which I also had a hand in, for at a very early age I used to help scrape and 'caulk' the wherry bottoms. The boatyard stopped making boats in the early days of the first world war and tried to become a pig and poultry farm, but there being so much lead paint about many animals died. Reeds were then stored there for paper making. It was only after my gandfather's death that the place was sold and it once more became a boatyard, as it is today.

The Wheelwright's Shop Bunwell 1906

Our uncle was a wheelwright and in these days when everything is machine-made, and the individual worker only performs one small routine operation, it may be of interest to recall the work of a real craftsman. Immediately to your right as you entered the white five-barred gate was the saw-pit. Behind this were stacked the straight tree trunks from which would eventually be fashioned a gentleman's smart trap, a tradesman's delivery van or a strong heavy tumbril for farm work.

Next came the woodshop, a large building with windows down each side and work-benches running its full length beneath. There were vice-like clamps at each end and an orderly array of tools was ranged at the back between windows and the working surface. Every size of chisel, of awl, screwdriver and plane was there, with graded saws on hooks, each in its own niche and in perfect condition. Woe betide the hapless apprentice who forgot to clean a tool or to return it to its proper place!

On your left as you walked towards the house was the forge—a place of joyous terror to two rather timid little girls when the boy worked at the bellows, making the sparks fly and the coals roar white-hot, whilst Uncle held an iron wheel-rim in the long tongs and beat it into shape with his heavy hammer.

Opposite the doorway of the forge, the grass had been hollowed out to form a shallow basin the size of a cart wheel with a flat boarded edge. On this the wooden wheel of the trap or tumbril was laid whilst the new iron rim with its white-hot joint was fitted. When this was satisfactorily in place, it was beaten together and then rapidly cooled by water from a long-spouted watering-can to make it contract. We watched from a safe distance and the hissing clouds of steam were, for us, the crowning thrill of that day's spectacular!

Beyond the forge was the Paint Shop, the holy of holies, with regularly sluiced down tiled floor and row upon row of paint cans, varnish, turpentine, brushes and all the paraphernalia of the finishing art. We were not allowed in the paint-shop lest we 'raise a dust'. So, of course, curiosity drew us to slip inside when no grown-ups were in sight, only to hear Uncle's voice shouting from the wood-shop: 'Hi, bor, what you doing thar?' Like so many Norfolk men he was bi-lingual, speaking the Queen's English when he chose but falling back into a much more expressive dialect to galvanise bad girls into convulsive action.

On a fine morning after rain in the night, the saw-pit was our great delight. One could sit on the flat-boarded edge of the seven foot deep oblong hole and watch the antics of the hordes of frogs and toads who had their lairs amongst the weeds sprouting from the crevices in its boarded sides. Sometimes we would assist their gymnastics with a small pebble thrown with considerable accuracy to land immediately behind, but never *on* the amusing creatures. When sawing was in progress, the long tree trunk was laid across the top of the pit and Uncle stood astride above it grasping the top handle of the great long saw on which the lad pulled from below. We pondered little in those days upon the skill of a craftsman's hands, but today it seems remarkable that those powerful arms and hands which controlled that great saw so that it cut along a pencilled line with unswerving accuracy, could also lay the long-bristled paint brush with exquisite delicacy to draw the fine lines of colour along the spokes of an elegant wheel or print free hand in fine lettering 'George Smith, Butcher, Forncett.' on a smart delivery van.

Brickmakers (i) Treading the clay Sprowston 1910

At a very early age I had to hurry home from school to take my neighbour's 'fourses', which usually consisted of a bottle of warm tea and some cakes, made like short cakes but fried in fat, instead of the usual baking method.
My neighbour worked at a Brickyard and I was never tired of watching the men working. They worked in bare feet with their trousers tied with string at the knees. Some of the men used to tread ('Jam it' was their expression) the clay mixture until it was just right to make bricks. This mixture was then taken in barrows to other men, who were standing in round pits about two or three feet deep, and here the mixture was put in wooden moulds, the surplus being smoothed off with a flat wooden board, and the moulded brick was turned out on slats round the pit (the process was similar to children making sand pies at the seaside). Other men would then come to collect the bricks and it was amazing to see these men running up a narrow plank in bare feet with a barrow load of bricks and not slipping over the edge, to pack

them into the kiln for burning, but before burning they were left for some days to partially weather dry.

(ii) The One-Man Kiln Foulsham 1920

Not far from our farm was a brick kiln long since out of use. This was a fascinating place in charge of an old gentleman who made the bricks from clay and put them in rows outside to dry and woe betide any cat walking along them leaving his footprints. When he had made thousands of them they were barrowed into the kiln to be fired. Everyone knew when this was happening as large clouds of smoke belched from the top of the kiln. It was terribly hot inside and the bricks took a few days to bake. When they had cooled the lovely red bricks were brought out ready for the builders to collect. The firing of the kiln happened about twice a year.

The Drayman Norwich 1910

My father was, at that time, a teetotaller, but when he became a drayman to Youngs, Chawslay and Youngs, he began to like the smell and taste of beer and I sometimes wonder how many gallons he must have drunk in the forty-eight years he worked for that firm. His basic wage when I was a child was twenty-one shillings with so much bonus added for empties he brought back and for the length of the journeys he made to deliver the beer, bringing his wage up to round about thirty shillings; this sum was quite good in those days.

During my summer school holidays I would go with my father all round Norfolk with the beer and many times we would be travelling home late at night and would pass no traffic of any sort. Probably we would both fall asleep and the horses would know their way home. We would wake up with the clatter of their hooves on the iron weigh bridge in the stable yard. I would hurry home and leave my father to feed and water the horses. My mother would be waiting to serve the evening meal; this would consist in the spring of spring cabbage boiled with light dumplings on top and served with melted butter. We could not afford much meat in those days but my father was very fond of this meal. Nowadays the publican pays for the beer by cheque or to the traveller, but in those days the draymen were paid in golden sovereigns and how I loved counting that money when he reached home: it would have been quite a haul for any would-be robbers in those days, but I don't ever remember his being short of any money.

We supplied our own entertainment and the evenings we enjoyed most were when my father taught us to dance. He would pull his thick woollen stockings over his trousers so that he looked a cross between a Volga boatman and a ballet dancer. In the summer we danced outside and during the winter indoors, but only if my father's eyes twinkled. This would mean he had had a certain amount of beer, making him rather merry. The only music we had was played by my father on a jews-harp, a lyre-shaped instrument placed between the teeth when being played.

From Bicycle Shop to Car Hire Aylsham 1907-1918

In 1907, my father opened a cycle shop in the little town. Farming people and others were just beginning to appreciate the advantages of being mobile on two slender wheels, and as my father's shop was the only one in a very wide area, business was brisk .

When I was about five, my father fashioned my first bicycle from a larger frame and taught me to ride it in the streets, lanes and country roads almost empty of traffic. They were practically dirt tracks, and one remembers the pleasures (and hazards!) of riding on tarred surfaces when they appeared. Many of my friends of those early days learned to balance on my little 'bike' and it brought my father much business.

Business improved and we moved to larger premises which would accommodate cars for hire (the first in the district) with bicycles fast becoming a side-line.

Then came the First World War. Mounted troops were billetted in the town. The cars were in great demand to take the soldiers to and from leave or to Norwich for an evening out.

Uses for Steam Aylsham 1920

In those days Mr Soames' foundry was very flourishing. My father was an engineer and went to work for Mr Soames when he returned from the War. The first steam roundabout had been made at this foundry and an Aylsham man took it on the road to show the fair people how to drive it. Mr Soames afterwards invented and built a motor car which was worked by steam.

A Use for Gunpowder Aylsham 1910

Whenever a wedding took place gunpowder used to be fired from the anvil at Crane Bros, (which is now a motor garage but in those days it was where they did the horse shoeing), in order to give the newly-weds a good wish.

School

Within living memory, there was a time when the summit of academic achievement was to be bright enough to leave school at the earliest possible age. And judging from some of the descriptions of village schools there was not much to attract children to stay longer than necessary. Like the clothes they wore, schooling for children at the turn of the century was not designed to be comfortable or liberating.

The Bucket in the Playground Southrepps 1880

My mother, now aged ninety-seven, recalls that during her early school days the only drinking water for the children at Southrepps School was a bucket of water which stood at the foot of a tree in the playground with a tin mug attached by a chain to the tree. Each child used this mug as needed.
The school fees at this time were twopence a week. Heating arrangements were inadequate, consisting of coal fires which seemed to be banked up with coal dust and only began to glow when it was time for the children to go home.

The Cost of Schooling Burgh St Peter 1884

I remember starting school at four years old, with my two elder brothers, with our dinner packed in a basket, and sixpence for our education. That was threepence for the eldest, twopence for the second and one penny for myself. My slate and pencil cost threepence. The governess was dressed in a brown dress with a large check, with a huge bustle behind, which I thought would be lovely to ride on.

School Leavers at eleven Filby 1890

Children could leave school when they were eleven years of age, providing they had a job, had made three hundred consecutive attendances for five years and were in Standard V. Many walked four miles to school; they had no milk, no hot dinners, and were very poor. T.B. was very bad and many children died.

The Long Walk Blakeney 1890

At the top of the High Street was the Church Primary School attended by the children from Blakeney, Wiveton and Glandford, the latter having to walk four miles there and four miles back every day. There was no water in the School for either drinking or washing.

'And Good Riddance Too' Knapton 1894

My father, now aged eighty-eight, tells me; 'School I couldn't stick, it cost a penny a week to go. When I was twelve I asked Miss Cooper, the teacher, if I could leave as I'd got myself a job. She said, 'Yes, and good riddance too'. I couldn't read or write then, but I learnt myself over the years.'

The Cane Spooner Row 1910

I do not remember a lot about early school, although I do remember the humiliating experience of standing in front of the class and receiving the stroke of the cane on both hands from the Headmaster, Mr Williams, for misbehaving in class after having been warned. We always wore white embroidered pinafores, I remember, to keep our frocks clean. These were fashioned from a yoke which fastened at the back with buttons and buttonholes and had large frills on the shoulders.

The Cane and Free Dinners Norwich 1910

The junior school I attended was a mixed school but when I reached the seniors, this was all girls and the boys went to another school. The cane was widely used and I received my share of it chiefly through being such a chatterbox.
We were always well fed, perhaps with rather more starch than was good for us, but Mother was a wonderful cook and house-

keeper. There was one nourishing sweet which used to arrive on the table looking like a huge snowball: boiled rice in a cloth; how I hated it if the golden syrup was rather scarce! There were school dinners and I, being one of a large family, could have had free dinners but I couldn't lower my pride in accepting anything free. I also heard that boiled rice in water was sometimes served. This turned me completely from having school dinners.

The Workhouse Children Aylsham 1910

The School, built in 1848 is still being used in 1970, with extensive interior modernisation. Boys and girls in my day were segregated and most girls wore mid-calf length dresses and pinafores.
Those coming from the Workhouse were scrubbed and clean and smelled of carbolic soap; they wore dresses of thick grey flannel and the pinafores were of coarse grey calico with 'Aylsham Union' printed across the back yokes in large purple letters.

Slates and Spit Aylsham 1910

In those very early school days, slates and slate pencils were in daily use for writing and arithmetic and it was common practice for 'spit' to be used in the process of cleaning. Collected after each lesson, and re-issued willy-nilly there was little regard for hygiene. Oh, the joy of having lined exercise books and pencils of one's own! Later, there were pens to dip in ink, often with disastrous consequences.

The Village School South Creake 1913

My earliest memories are centred round the village school at South Creake, to which I was admitted in 1913 when not quite five years old.
I well remember how the blazing sun and dusty main road were left behind when we opened the tall red door in the high wall and stepped into the dim coolness of the Girls' and Infants' playground. The huge beech tree with its silvered bole and spreading roots stood in the centre and shed a dappled light over all. To the left, the long school building cast a deep shadow and immediately

opposite the Beck formed the north boundary as it rippled over its stony bed. A row of alder trees grew at the edge, their gnarled roots dipping into its cool depths, whilst catkins and tiny black cones dropped into the swirling eddies.

At the right hand side of the playground door, discreetly screened behind maroon corrugated iron, were the 'Offices'. Six bucket closets with wooden seats of ascending heights served the Infants and the Girls, whilst a latrine at the far end, for the Infant boys boasted a drain which dripped constantly into the Beck. This area was slightly noisesome, but country children like their parents are supposed to be accustomed to strong smells.

The long, low brick-built Infants' and Girls' cloakroom was at the far end of the playground at right angles to the main building. Inside, the walls and a centre wooden partition were crammed with a double row of coat pegs. The older girls used the upper pegs, whilst the smaller children hung their clothes on the lower ones, or threw them on the floor to be trodden on. When the school bell rang, the cloak room was a congested mass of squiggling bodies.

The door of the Infants' class room was on the left. Miss X, a young, quick, shrill-voiced, sharp-tempered uncertificated teacher was in charge. To this day I can see her pounce upon an inattentive child, push up his sleeves and smack his arm until it became red and tears rolled down his cheeks.

Fortunately, I was in the Babies' class in the care of a quiet, kindly soul who, having no training in the art of school teaching, was called a Supplementary Teacher and addressed as Teacher Milly. The privilege of holding her hand was so greatly prized that her progress to and from school was impeded by a string of children on either side.

On the south wall of the long Infants' classroom were four tall, narrow windows which looked out on to the Boys' playground at the front of the school. The walls were of that shade of green considered most soothing to the eyes. Oil lamps hung from the high ceiling and gave light on winter afternoons and distributed globules of oil on those below all the year round. The fireplace was in the long wall opposite the windows and was surrounded by a massive iron guard on which damp clothes were hung to dry on wet days, and round which we clustered at play time to warm our frozen fingers.

The wooden desks were long and narrow and each seated six squirming Infants. The lids could be raised, but the seats were fixed and this necessitated an entry with bent knees. Pencils and papers were scarce in those days and we wrote with wooden skewers in shallow trays of sand. Any mistakes could easily be obliterated in the shifting sand, and so could a whole morning's toil. If an unfortunate inmate dropped his skewer, crawled down to the floor to retrieve it and ascended with doubled back, he would invariably raise the lid of the long, long desk, jolt all the sand trays and a morning's work could be lost in oblivion. I have been told that when I first went to school, I knew all my letters, and my father had patiently taught me to repeat the alphabet not only forwards, but backwards. However, this accomplishment was of little value to me for Miss X was so up-to-date that she had discarded the alphabetic system of learning to read and Teacher Milly had to introduce us to the mysteries of the Phonic system. At home, as I struggled with phonetics, my dismayed parents thought I was swearing.

There were no individual reading books for the Babies' class. We worked from a wall chart, following Teacher Milly's pointer and repeating the sounds collectively. The slow learners found this a great advantage, for their voices were submerged beneath those of the sharper ones, and as there was no evidence that they had not understood, they escaped retribution.

Besides learning to read and write, we spent part of each day in varied occupations to give us manual dexterity, though of course we were not aware of this. Threading beads was most enjoyed. The colours were so brilliant. As we sucked the threading lace to a sharper point, and induced it to penetrate the hole, we felt a sense of achievement at the capture of another victim, and watched it slide down the lace to join its brilliant companions. Sometimes, as an aid to counting, we were asked to thread in numbered groups. Then there was Fraying or Frazzling or Unravelling threads from pieces of material to make stuffing for cushions: and of course there was the never ending joy of clay or Plasticine modelling. We could create anything which caught our fancy, though it did leave our little hands greasy and smelly, but these could be washed in the Beck and dried on our petticoats.

During the day, there would be communal lessons at which the Babies joined the Infants. We sang lustily though somewhat tunelessly, accompanied by Teacher Milly on the wheezy harmonium, or played chasing games, or skipping in the playground. Sometimes the two teachers took us for walks in a long crocodile to gather wild flowers or berries, or watch the blacksmith shoeing the horses or blowing up the red hot forge with the bellows. In Springtime we went to the farm to see the young lambs, or to the dairy to watch the farmer's wife skim the cream from the flat round pans of milk or turn the churn to make butter. I presume this was to get us talking and enlarge our vocabulary.

If we wished to visit the Offices during lessons, we raised a hand and asked: 'Please teacher, may I leave the room?' Miss X being unable to distinguish dire need from sheer boredom, invariably refused and faced the consequences.

Teacher Milly never attempted to discriminate but sent us flying immediately across the playground accompanied by a friend to help with our buttons. For in the days before elastic was in common use the fullness of our calico drawers was gathered into two waistbands, with a button-hole at each end. The front band was fastened over buttons at the side of the stays, and the back band over the same two buttons. When 'paying a visit', it was only necessary to let down the back flap, and not lower the whole garment. All this occupied some time, for besides re-fastening the buttons, with one's petticoats and dress bunched up under the arms, one could examine and admire the lace or embroidery on the knee-bands of the knickers and then wander back across the yard.

Eventually, I went up into Miss X's class where I presume I progressed favourably, for I do not remember any punishments, though I can distinctly remember being allowed to knit a pair of reins, seated in front of the class, whilst teacher gave extra tuition to the backward readers.

As Infants, we had little contact with the rest of the school, except for the older children who delivered us safely each morning and afternoon and collected us duly dressed for home at the end of each session.

Which are the lucky ones? Shotesham 1900

We had to be tough those days trudging to school in all weathers. How lucky the children are today, or are they? We had lots of fun.

The Private School Foulsham 1928

Over the sideboard hung the painting of a young lad. Arrogant, arresting and sensual, portrayed as only the true artist can. One felt the intimacy of painter and poser. I admired the painting and asked who had painted it. 'A. M. Priest. You must remember Miss Priest, she taught you.' Indeed I did.

I remembered an autocratic, Victorian spinster who ruled my life for five years. I could not in any way reconcile the painter of the gypsy lad with the maiden lady who taught me the three R's. She lived in an age when there was no livelihood to be gained from painting, so in order to maintain two elderly dependent parents she had had to run a private school.

The School was held in a Georgian fronted house. Elegant whitened steps led up to the pillared front door. Never in all the five years that I attended the school do I remember using that front door. We skulked in a narrow alley between the houses until ten to nine, or ten to two when a side door was left ajar for us to enter as silently as possible. Once inside we wiped our feet assiduously on the mat inside the door. Then we changed our shoes in a small stoneflagged room. This was our playroom. Although there was a large untidy garden behind the house we were never allowed in it. Our playroom was unheated and sunless, the window net-shrouded and filled with geraniums.

Here we stayed until rescued by an exalted eleven-year-old who was monitor for the week. This important personage would have been into the classroom to put out the pens, pencils, inkwells, and to have opened the piano and found the hymn. We were conducted silently down a long passage, dark and smelling of damp, to the classroom.

The classroom had once been the drawing room of the house. The red and blue carpet was covered with a white drugget which had to remain unmarked from beginning of term to the end. Any spots, a mark of reproach to the delinquent and punishable by the dire Conduct mark. Over the fireplace, modestly draped with a green fringed overmantel was a large gold framed mirror. Stuck into the frame of the mirror were two peacock feathers, so much a part of the scene that it is only on looking back that I question their presence.

The piano to whose accompaniment we raggedly sang the morning hymn was a maze of fret work over faded rose silk. The wood was a knotted walnut of unbelievable grain.

Miss Priest sat centre stage at a large table while we occupied various desks according to size about the room.

The room had one window, again heavily draped, which looked on to the village street. I could tell the passing of the day by the villagers outside. The succession of men to the barber's nearby ended with the butcher at ten thirty; the baker's carts left the bakery and rattled past next. Twice a week the fish cart bell would herald the approach of twelve o'clock.

The long drowsy afternoon ended with the return of the mill carts, the old horses slathering at their loose flaccid mouths. Their return coincided with the shouts of the children from the Primary School as they were released, some of them setting out on a two mile walk to neighbouring villages. I do not remember any feeling of sympathy at their long, often cold and wet walk ahead, only a feeling of envy that they were released fifteen long minutes before us. I tried for five long years to acquire a fair hand of writing, without success. I copied the beautiful script that Miss Priest wrote in my exercise books. I worked my way through six printed copy books but legibility always escaped me. I applied myself to the hieroglyphics of Arithmetic, adding parrot fashion. I learned my tables and eventually mastered fractions and decimals without being in any way aware of the propensities of either. I read my way solidly through endless history and geography books none of which in any way fired my imagination. The one thing I did learn, and when I saw the gypsy boy I knew why, I learned to paint.

I learned the glories of mixing paint. Blues and yellows and a touch of burnt sienna became the colour of a leaf fresh uncurled.

Red and blue, and I had a purple of royal hue. I learned too before I was ten the meaning of perspective.
I see again that figure I feared so much; the dress of black bombazine, the modesty vest and seed pearl brooch. The hair scraped back so tightly it seemed to draw her very face with it, that face that never smiled and certainly never laughed. I see and now I understand. How she must have hated teaching the succession of children who passed through her hands. How she must have longed for the sun and scenery. How much talent wasted in those chilblained hands. How was I to know there were two of us hating that classroom.

Teaching as a career (i) 1887

A memory Mother treasured was of being taught by Edith Cavell in the Sunday School at Swardeston Church. When she was sixteen in 1887 Mother went as a pupil teacher to Carrow School in Norwich, built for the children of employees of J. and J. Colman by Jeremiah Colman, founder of the firm. She taught all elementary subjects, and in the evenings prepared lessons and studied for her teaching certificate.

(ii) 1917

I made up my mind that I would like to take up teaching as a career. I started my apprenticeship as a Student Teacher for a year prior to training. I was put in charge of a small class in a rural area, having to cope with children of all ages. Periodically we had families of gypsies in the district, the children of whom were forced by law to attend the local school if resident in one place for more than a fortnight. These visits did much to relieve the monotony of the curriculum. On one occasion a babe-in-arms arrived carried by one of the bigger girls. She could not attend school without the baby, as mother was out peddling pegs. Then one of the boys was very surprised at being stopped from chasing another with an open jack-knife with which he intended to settle an argument.
Later, I moved to another rural school and really enjoyed my stay

there, in spite of parents who would not let me keep their offspring when they needed extra tuition in arithmetic. 'For,' said Father, 'he dorn't want ter know that to drive a plough.'

The Village Schoolmaster (i) Shipdham 1917

The schoolmaster, next to the policeman was the most feared man in the village. He was the only psychiatrist we knew. He and his cane could sort anybody out. Juvenile delinquents didn't exist. Only boys and girls—none perfect—but some worse than others. We sat on forms in class with our arms folded tightly behind our backs. Hands were not allowed to stray in front. The classroom was heated with a coal fire and the schoolmaster invariably stood with his back to the fire. 'Deep freeze' meant my feet.

(ii) Matlaske 1919

1919, and the soldiers returned home. Our school served four villages and in each the leading farmer gave a 'Welcome Home' feast. Beer flowed freely and it was a real 'Barn Dance'. We girls, the schoolmaster's daughters, went to all four and my sisters took turns in playing the piano for dancing—the polka 'A-hunting we will go' and 'Sir Roger' and for songs—'My little grey home'—'A long, long trail' and 'Tipperary'.

In the midst of the singsong the big double doors of the barn opened and my father who had come to walk his daughters home, stood silhouetted. The cry went up 'Here come a-measter' as my father, white haired and a little bent, gravely saluted grown men whose backsides he had tanned when they were boys and he was red-haired, bearded and erect.

Getting about

Everything that can be said has been said about the effect, both distance-shrinking and peace-destroying, of the motorcar in our lives. So let us think instead of those exciting travel experiences that we shall never have again—the carrier's cart, the ponytrap, the bone-shaker bicycle, the steam train, the tram, the *first* motorbus and the *first* motorcar. But we still have feet, and perhaps we shall learn to use them again as our ancestors did, when the roads finally seize up with cars.

Not getting about Wood Norton 1910

In those days the village was very self-contained, regarding anybody living beyond its boundaries as a 'foreigner'. London was only a name, except to the rich and adventurous few; Norwich was seldom visited and only Fakenham was known by all. This was the market town seven miles away, to which many of the farm workers walked to spend their harvest wages. As late as 1925 my husband, then in his teens and daring to visit a girl in the neighbouring village of Swanton Novers received a message, threatening that if he 'didn't keep to his own place he would be stoned home'. There was at least one family at the school who had never seen the sea, just twelve miles away, nor had they ever travelled by railway train.

They couldn't afford to ride Horstead 1912

The Aunt I visited at Horstead told of how before buses or trains, she and her husband walked seven miles each way whenever they visited Norwich, sometimes even pushing a pram. It was in this way she spent her last hours with her husband who was emigrating to Australia to make a home for her and their family. They could not afford to ride. Alas, he never returned, but left her a widow (after an accident) with six children to rear.

The Carrier's Cart (i) Drayton to Norwich 1910

We used to go to Norwich sometimes, mostly when my Granny got her Co-op Dividend. A Carrier's Cart used to pass our gate twice a week. It was rather like a Black Maria with seats all round it and all sorts of goods piled on the floor to be delivered in Norwich. The driver put up at the Artichoke Inn. But when money was short, my Granny and I sometimes walked to Norwich. We got rather tired on the way back and used to play 'I spy' and such games to help us along. We lived half-way between Drayton and Hellesdon.

(ii) To Lynn Mart 1910

We went to Lynn Mart in the Carrier's Van. After trying each ride and seeing the sideshows, we made our way home in the same way stopping at almost every house. My mother called the carrier's wife a 'masterpiece'. She knew everyone's sizes from top to toe, how many rolls of paper for each room, the curtain yardage for each window, and how much to give for it to suit each family. The weather for these visits was always Mart Weather—bitter winds with snow and frost.

(iii) Aylsham to Norwich 1910

Sometimes on a Saturday I would visit my grandmother in Norwich riding in the Carrier's Cart. This carrier went from Aldeburgh through Aylsham, and on these occasions I would be waiting at the New Inn 7.30 a.m. and put in charge of the driver. Later when I used to read about David Copperfield riding in a carrier's cart with Barkis, I knew just how he felt.

(iv) Norwich to Shipdham 1906

One of my Dad's workmates invited my sister and me to be his bridesmaids. After the wedding the bridegroom's Mother said, would I like to spend my Summer holiday with her in the Country? The Country was a completely unknown place to me called Shipdham.

I eagerly accepted, arrangements were made and I longed for the next few weeks to pass. At last the Saturday did arrive. I was to go by Carrier's Cart from St Benedicts. Only the older Norwich people will know this, but just past Barn Road was a wide opening between two Public Houses, St Benedicts had dozens then. This was the place where country folk met for their transport to the various villages outside Norwich every week. Mother and I were there by two o'clock and I took my seat, but the driver appeared from the depths of the adjoining rowdy and beer singing places after four o'clock. By that time the Carrier's Cart was crammed full of humans and boxes, parcels of every size, not to mention a dog or two. My luggage consisted of a Japanese basket contraption, two lids overlapping each other, secured with a strap outside (forerunner of our expanding suitcases of today). The Carrier's Cart was a covered waggon affair—seats all round and across, and was pulled all the way by one horse. It was quite pleasant at first, although I could not see a thing of the scenery, as I was sitting at the back on a very hard board in this covered waggon affair, and it was Plonk Plonk Plonk for miles ever more. Sometimes we stopped to drop folks and parcels and then other passengers got on. I know it was quite dark when we arrived and I was feeling so homesick, tired and hungry.

My hostess was waiting for me—so this was the Country: a dark place, no street lights, no parks. I just longed to get to bed and wake up to find I was with my sisters and mother. It all proved to be entirely different in the morning and I had a very happy holiday.

The Village Cab Gimingham 1920

The nearest station was three miles away, but if anybody wanted to travel there was Tammy's Cab. Tammy himself had been retired ever since I could remember anything. He spent his days snoozing in front of his kitchen fire. The horse who was about the same age snoozed in the stable, and the cab and the hens occupied the shed next door. Calls upon Tammy were few, but were taken by his wife, who wrote them on a slate which she kept behind the clock on the mantelpiece. Tammy couldn't bring himself to take notes as 'he never had no book larning'. At the appropriate moment Mrs Tammy woke him up, and then went into the stable to wake up the horse. Some time had to be allowed to get them both saddled and collected. Frequently one or both would drop off again before the destination was reached.

Railways and the Station Fly Aylsham 1907

I remember when I first came to Norfolk. The century was just seven years old, and a child of four found life very exciting. Born at Lowestoft, coming to Norfolk meant a journey in a great black clattering monster, belching steam, and what a thrill it was.
At the end of that ride, came another shorter one, in a kind of box on wheels with padded seats inside, facing each other. This was known as the 'Station Fly', and being horse-drawn, provided yet another thrill on that memorable day, especially as a small girl was allowed to give the horse a lump of sugar, when we finally arrived.
A coach and horses still plied between Norwich and Cromer for a short while after we arrived, and a Carrier's Cart travelled to more remote country districts on two days each week. There was a railway station at each end of the town. At the north end was the Midland and Great Northern railway carrying trains to Great Yarmouth and Lowestoft from the Midlands and North.
In summer, excursion trains with a dozen or even more coaches, would rattle through without stopping, each coach packed tight with laughing, shouting crowds of holiday makers. The Great Eastern Railway provided a handy and comparatively comfortable link with the City of Norwich, for many small towns and villages. Alas! In 1970 the M. and G.N. is little more than a grass track in places, and on the old G.E.R. line an occasional diesel-powered engine draws along a few goods trucks.

Holiday Coach and Horses Aylsham 1910

I once remarked 'Coach and Horses' in a conversation and the query came, 'You surely cannot remember them?' The one I remembered used to go from Cromer to Norwich during the summer season. The horses were changed at the Black Boys—in those days a real coaching Inn. We would hurry from school in the afternoon to see the coach leave for Cromer and the passengers would throw pennies to us. As the coach went down the Market and Red Lion Street the postillion would blow his long horn, not to clear the way, for you could walk anywhere in the market and streets in a leisurely fashion without fear of being run over.

The Pony Cart Norwich 1910

I remember some happy childhood outings before World War One. My father, although a Norwich business man could handle a horse and cab or pony cart. Nowadays this seems strange, but cars were only just coming into use and the alternative was by train. Whether others used horse drawn vehicles themselves I can't remember, but I had rather a smug feeling seeing my father sitting up there puffing his pipe and jogging along.
Sometimes we went to Ringland Hills. The horse my father hired was never too lively in case it bolted with us, so when we reached the steepest hills we all had to get out and walk, thus the horse didn't become too exhausted. On arrival at the top of the incline we had tea and the horse ate from a nosebag of oats.

The Governess Car Norwich 1910

We would go to Church on Sunday in the Governess Car, and there was a long iron bar outside to which the ponies were tethered.

Bicycles (i) The Hired Bone-Shaker Horstead 1915

Having reached my teens I was elevated to a monstrosity we called a 'Bone-Shaker' hired from a character called 'Dodger' who also sold buckets of coal for a few pence. My steed cost sixpence per hour, so I lost as little time as possible on the seven mile journey to Horstead.

(ii) Carbide Lamps Great Moulton 1930

When I was a child I loved to be pushed along on the seat of an aunt's bicycle. Sitting up there seemed almost tree level, for cycles in those days were very high with straight handlebars and large wheels. The ladies had to be careful not to get their dresses caught in the wheels. There were coloured string dress guards, like a second lot of spokes around the back wheel to help to protect their clothes.

One of my Uncles had a carbide lamp for his bicycle and I can still smell the pungent gas which issued from it when he got it ready for use.

(iii) When it was safe to cycle Norwich 1910

I was given a bicycle on my thirteenth birthday. Very few cars were seen on the roads at that time, and my friends and I could cycle quite safely through the country lanes. We went for picnics on Ringland Hills, or on one of the many Commons around Norwich. In later years we cycled to the sea, and thought we were fashionable in our knee-length bathing costumes.

The Steam Car Aylsham 1920

After the War my father worked at Mr Soames' foundry. Mr Soames invented and built a motorcar which was worked by steam. Mr Soames sat in the back and drove while my father sat in front to steer. It had wooden wheels with iron tyres and a tin roof—it was sure a sight to behold travelling along the road. While out on a journey the steam would become low after a few miles and it would be necessary to stop by the roadside. The driver had to beg water from friendly folk and wait until the water boiled before the journey could be resumed. The noise was terrific, but it was a wonderful achievement.

The Tramcar Norwich 1910

Sometimes my father would take my brother and me to Pulls Ferry. We would cross the river in the Ferry Boat, go by tramcar to Thorpe Road terminus, walk to Whitlingham Station and return to Norwich by train. It was an afternoon treat for us.
The old tramcars had an open top reached by a narrow iron stairway and in wet weather the journey was very unpleasant. I wonder what one of our prominent City Councillors would have said, if he had known of the tramcars' disappearance from the streets. He disapproved of them and used to rap his cane on every tram post as he walked along.

The Weekly Bus (i) Great Moulton 1930

Most villages had a once weekly or even once daily bus which went to Norwich when I was small. This not only took passengers but also luggage on a rack on the roof.
Sometimes live chickens were in crates amongst the parcels or a cycle for one of the passengers to return from Norwich at a more convenient time than the bus did. One of these buses found it difficult to get up a hill just outside Norwich and this would be the signal for the passengers to get out and push, but I don't think that there was a reduction in fare for this service. In spite of all this I remember being thrilled at the prospect of a trip to Norwich by bus.

(ii) Blakeney to Norwich 1920's

Our means of transport were very limited indeed. Those who had not their own horses hired Mr Pye's waggonette or pony trap. When there was enough snow on the roads we used a horse-sledge, the winters being much colder than now. The first motor-bus ever to run to Norwich had an awning over it, and forms to sit on—fare three and sixpence return. The bus was driven by Mr Heseltine of Cley, who did errands for 'old girls' as we went along. I remember at one cottage the owner was standing outside and called out: 'Ha ye got my neighbour's umberrelly?' Another when asked where she wished to get out answered: 'Du yu put me down, bor, where you picked up my niece last year.' Mr Heseltine was expected to remember everyone and all their doings. On the return journey it was quite usual to be sitting next to a half-side of bacon instead of a passenger.

The First Car (i) The Dust Marsham

I can remember just seeing the first motor car that came through Marsham—the vision was partly blurred owing to the amount of white dust which covered the roads in those days.

(ii) Watching it go by Saxlingham

I can also remember the first Motor Car that came to the village—folk used to go on to the road to watch it go by—a real thrill.

(iii) In the Dickie Spooner Row

My first car ride I remember was when I was about 13 years old in the Dickie seat of the car of the then Vicar of Wymondham, Rev S. Martin Jones, who brought three of us home one summer evening—a matter of three miles from having attended a Bible Class at the vicarage. It was a great thrill for us.

(iv) The 'Guvner's' Flying Machine Gimingham

My father, always anxious to keep abreast of the times, bought a motor car, a fearsome looking brute with a lot of brass everywhere. It made a terrible noise, and was spoken of as the 'guvner's' flying machine. He was also the first in the village to instal a wireless, and as the tall aerial pole was being fixed at the end of the stables old Jimma was heard to say rather disdainfully: 'How do the guvner think he's a'goin' to shin up that there pole to hear that there old stuff.'

Wherries and Lighters (i) Aylsham 1910

The Wherries used to come down the Bure to the Staithe and we children would walk on the narrow ledge of the boat. Some friends of mine who lived at Dunkirk at the time told me they used to walk along the river bank to the lock and the wherryman would let them ride back on the Wherry to the Staithe.

(ii) Pentney

Pentney was a small scattered village only accessible over water. I recall when Pentney Mill was the Toll-bridge and the horses and carts trundled to Marham by the bridle roads. Now all are gone for ever.
The Lighters used to travel with the bones from King's Lynn to the Bone Mill along the River Nar, to be ground as bone meal for use on the land.
A Public House stood at the Mill where the Lightermen could have a night's lodging. Pentney once boasted five Public Houses. Now there's only one.

Part Five

Norfolk

Places People Events

Places

This peaceful county

The sails gliding through fields, no water, no boat, just sails—elegant, mysterious, the huge expanse of sky, the sunsets. . . . The intangible something that drew us back year after year to the quiet beauty, clear healing air of this peaceful county has now succeeded in claiming for good the 'old folks' who have come to spend the rest of their days surrounded by the rolling fields, the haunting cry of the seagull, the flowers, the peace, the friendships, all started so long ago by a Norfolk holiday which I remember so well.

Foxing the furriners

I remember when we moved to Norfolk, away back in the thirties. We had come some hundreds of miles, only to be lost when we crossed into Norfolk, in the maze of lanes and roads. I feel sure it's the only county with signposts with the same name pointing in two different directions. Later on when our visitors came we had many a laugh. We would give them explicit directions, to which they paid no heed, until the day arrived when they were coming to us, then they wished they had.

Blakeney 1890's

Leaving the Manor House one passed the sail-makers shed, where the Community Centre now stands, and the old Guild-hall, which in those days was used as a mortuary for anyone drowned at sea. There is an underground passage from the Guild-hall under the hill believed to go to Wiveton Hall.

On leaving the Guild-hall if you climbed up the Mariners Hill you would get a lovely view of the harbour, and if it happened to be high-tide would see a lovely sight of sailing ships—the 'Blue Jacket', or 'Mary-Ann', or 'Fiducia' with full sails. They were moored to the large posts on the quay, and these posts had to be kept in order by the owner of the manorial rights. In return each cargo-ship that tied up at the quay had to take two hundredweights of coal to the Manor House. After the ships were moored another peaceful sight would be the waggons drawn by four horses arriving with loads of corn from the neighbouring farms, to be loaded into the ships and taken to the North.

Passing on round the quay you could see two blacksmiths' shops, one on the quay and one in Pig Street—now called Westgate Street.

There were several small shops in the High Street, including two bakeries kept by T. and C. Russell where you could buy bread with lovely crisp crusts, also cakes and dumplings.

We also had two cobblers' shops where first-class handwork was done. We loved to take our shoes to be mended by Mr Coffin—his one remaining lock of hair was tied over the top of his head by a piece of cobbler's green string! We thought this most amusing.

Almost next door lived Billy Mann the Barber. My brother loved to go there to have his hair cut, as Billy had a wooden leg and this used to be dragged out from under the old sofa and fixed to his stump before beginning operations. Billy's fees were threepence, but one day my brother came home very delighted. Billy had snipped his ear so only charged him three halfpence. The remaining three halfpence he spent at Miss Pye's sweet shop on the opposite side of the street.

There was no Town and Country Planning in those days, and most of the houses had been built close together to give shelter from the wind, and mostly were in yards leading off the main street and called after the oldest inhabitant, or longest resident in the yard. Each yard possessed a communal well, and very hard work it was to draw the water as I remember when we afterwards lived at St Margaret's and had a well.

There was an excellent little Golf Course on The Eyot, with old Bob Dix as groundsman, followed by Lee, then Tom Cobon, who did wonderful work keeping the Links in order, working six days a week with no time restriction, often working late after matches. His wages were thirty shillings a week.

Great Yarmouth and Mundesley 1900

My father, now aged eighty-eight says: 'I can remember Great Yarmouth when the sea front was all beach, and at Mundesley the coal boats used to anchor a little way out and horses and carts used to go out to them and unload the coal up the roadway which is still there.'

Great Yarmouth 1920's

I remember in the autumn the happy faces of the Scotch fisher-girls preparing the herrings on the Quayside. The drifters made a splendid picture as they slowly wended their way into the harbour to empty their catches.

Poppy-land 1900-30

One summer day in 1922 I went for a char-à-banc ride from Cromer around Poppy-land. Along the coast road at Sidestrand, on the sides of the road and in the cornfields, were masses of scarlet poppies.

During the 1930's a Miss Jermy, an old woman carrying a very large heavy basket from which she was selling bunches of flowers and herbs, came to my door at Cromer. One day, after she had called a few times, I invited her in to rest awhile, as she looked weary. I asked her where she lived, and she told me that she lived at Sidestrand and, when a girl, was the miller's daughter mentioned in Clement Scott's book 'Poppy-land'.

Clement Scott, who was staying in the district in 1897, one day strolled to Sidestrand hoping to find somewhere to stay so that he could continue his visit. At a bend in the road on a slope was a windmill, and on the opposite side of the road a farmhouse where the miller lived. Clement Scott went to the house and asked:

'Could I be allowed a lodging for a few days?'

'Indeed you could,' the miller's daughter replied.

This incident is mentioned in Clement Scott's book 'Poppy-land', which is about Sidestrand and district. The book consists of what we reoriginally articles for a newspaper, probably the 'Daily

Telegraph', and did much to make the district widely known as 'Poppy-land'.

After that time, China with poppies on it—named Poppy-land china—was sold in gift shops for souvenirs.

One autumn day a relative and I, when out for a long walk from Cromer, called to see Miss Jermy who then lived in a cottage in Smuggler's Lane, Sidestrand, very near the edge of the cliff. She showed us the Poppy-land fancy dress she had worn when she was a girl. It was a long corn-coloured dress with poppies made of material sewn on it, and had become very faded with age.

Norwich 1900-1910

Norwich, where I spent many years of my early life, is full of memories as I walk its streets, now so rapidly changing. Most of those streets were paved with granite setts and the footpaths formed with stone slabs. I remember the smell of dust as the water cart sprinkled the streets on a hot summer day, the glow of gas-lights turned on one by one as the lamplighter with his pole advanced up the road in the dusk of the evening. I remember the sound of the horse buses clip-clopping through the city, with an extra horse to pull them up Guildhall Hill, until they were superseded by up-to-date trams running on lines with overhead wires. On these one could ride 'up top', where the seats were reversible and had black rubber aprons to protect one's knees from rain. The trams covered the main roads of the city, routes being indicated by coloured boards; the driver stood in front exposed to the weather, and in case of need he could drop a 'cow catcher', a useful adjunct on cattle market days.

Shops bore names of well-known 'city fathers', many of whom were Lord Mayors or Sheriffs in their time—Chamberlin, Bond, Garland, Curl, Copeman and Eddington were among them. Floors of the shops were rough boards, and there were high wooden counters with overhead 'tramways' conveying containers with the customer's payment to the cashier. Change soon came whizzing back, but as the price of nearly all draper's goods ended with three farthings, the purchaser was presented with a packet of pins in place of the farthing change. Assistants wore black dresses, and a shop walker in morning suit affably greeted customers. In the grocers' shops, sides of bacon hung from the ceiling, sacks of sugar and currants stood on the floor, dry goods were kept in canisters or drawers and weighed out as needed. Shops kept open until seven o'clock at night, and ten or eleven on Fridays and Saturdays. Highlights of the year were the Fat Cattle Show held before Christmas in the Agricultural Hall and the Trades Exhibition in the autumn. Everyone enjoyed this, chiefly because of the quantities of 'samples' one could collect, and for the fascinating Fairy Fountain with its rainbow-coloured dancing waters.

I recall the cries of the city—before daylight on Shrove Tuesday boys calling 'Hot Coquilles', and 'Hot Cross Buns' on Good Friday, on winter Sunday afternoons the muffin man ringing his bell to announce 'Hot muffins for tea!' In the early morning cries of 'Milko' would herald the progress along the street of the milk float with its patient horse, waiting while the milkman measured from his churn into jugs put out on doorsteps overnight.

Then the 'characters' of the city—how well I remember them—at St Giles' Gates the man turning the handle of his soundless phonograph with its notice, 'Kind friends, my organ is out' (why organ, I wondered?), the woman whose pitch was Castle Meadow who sang snatches of 'Count your Blessings' and alternately swore loudly at her dog. Best known of all was Billy Bluelight who frequented The Walk, selling a cure for all ills, or 'Lovely heather!' from Mousehold. He was a champion walker, and could walk to Yarmouth by road faster than the pleasure steamer 'Jenny Lind' could do the trip by river from Foundry Bridge. Barrel organ players with their little monkeys had their regular rounds, and we watched for the rag and bone men, who gave coloured paper windmills in exchange.

These are some of my happy memories, but I have many sad ones too. In the early years of the century there was much that made life a hard struggle for many. Wages were low, working hours long, lives shadowed by fear of sickness and unemployment, which might mean starvation. I have seen under-nourished children with ragged clothes and bare feet, old men sweeping mud from street crossings or holding horses' heads for the few pence thrown to them, aged people destitute and unwanted, whose only end was the workhouse. In Norwich I knew many courts and yards (Paradise Court, Flower-in-Hand Yard, Rising Sun Place—lovely names) where people lived in poverty in crowded tenements. Now these sad things are gone, and are only memories.

Shopping in Norwich 1912

We did most of our shopping in Magdalen Street. Frank Price's was such a friendly shop, and their goods were suitable for country people and made to last. A Mrs Attoe had a shop at Stump Cross and sold secondhand furniture as well as new. I expect she was the beginnings of the firm that is there today. A Mr Batterbee was a tailor there, and his son was the schoolmaster at Drayton School at that time. He died last year, aged ninety. Loose's was a long narrow shop then with piles of plates and other crockery on the floor. There was a cheap bazaar where I used to look at the toys. We used to have our dinner at an eating house, Grix's, at the Back of the Inns.

Cromer Beach and Henry Blogg 1925

With our small terraced house in the Suffield Park area of Cromer was included a hut on the East beach, and we have always been beach people. At times during my teens I rebelled against spending so much of the summer there (a phase repeated by my own children), but it has become the background and pattern of all our summers. To me, no beach can satisfy like that of Cromer. It is filled with past images of childhood cricket matches (to me enforced misery); catching shrimps and later listening to their dying leaps in the saucepan of boiling sea water; tennis on the hard sand with string and walking sticks for net; exploration of the sand-locked wreck of the 'Fernebo', a relic of the 1914 war; the time we buried very deeply my tall twelve-year-old cousin up to his neck in sand and then panicked when we could not release him and had to call his father to the rescue; the time a landslide pushed our hut to the edge of the promenade, and that when it was carried away by high seas.

On the beach at the East end of the promenade there used to be two rows of high-wheeled bathing machines, no longer horse-drawn but hired by bathers too modest to undress on the beach. To hire one of these or a canvas beach-hut, one contacted Henry Blogg, the famous lifeboat coxswain, whose headquarters were in another converted bathing machine at the foot of the Doctor's Steps slope. He was a quiet but friendly man, a truly modest hero. For some years he was always accompanied by a large, melancholy dog of the husky type, named Monte, which he had rescued from a wreck on which the dog's master had been drowned. Blogg's most famous rescue in my time was that of the 'Sepoy'. I was at school when the two men clung to the barge's rigging quite close to the shore until Blogg drove the lifeboat twice over the deck to rescue them. Next Saturday the 'Sepoy' with her cargo of red tiles still lay on the beach, and all the children explored her. She looked too small to go to sea.

Before the peace was shattered Hethel 1930-70

Some months ago I stood looking around on a vast area of concrete roadways. The buildings nearby consist of offices, and a factory which turns out world-famous racing cars.
Previously, during the second world war, on this same site there were different activities. There were runways, hangars, air-raid shelters, and massive Flying Fortresses, and huts housing a large number of the United States Air Force. Many heads were shaken doubtfully when this Air Station was started. Was it not some of the best wheat-growing land in Norfolk?
In spite of it all, woods were disposed of, two cottages were knocked down, hedges torn out, and in no time at all there emerged a first-class aerodrome. This happened all over Norfolk, and helped save our country from defeat, I know, but in one of those attractive, well-built cottages I spent part of my childhood. Our playground was the woods and meadows, the woods with such delightful names as 'The White Woman', 'North America', The Nut Wood' and the 'Tenacre', where grew the biggest blackberries I have ever seen, and wild strawberries, which tasted to us much better than those which we grew in the garden. There were

patches of lily of the valley, stretches of bluebells and other wild flowers, many of them rare.

All kinds of birds nested in one particular wood, and one of our privileges was to accompany our father on his rounds as a gamekeeper along the green well-kept woodland rides to the pheasant-rearing section, with strict instructions always to walk behind him, especially when he was carrying his gun.

We walked to school during the summer through flower-filled meadows leading to 'Bush Close', which in those days was a wooded tract of land near a by-road.

Whilst waiting for sleep during those long summer evenings we would hear the whirring notes of a nightjar coming from across the 'Pond Pightle', and more than one nightingale singing, with never a car or lorry to shatter the peace of it all.

Sometimes, after a visit to my relatives in Norwich, my home surroundings tended to make me feel lonely. I missed the city life and wished for more people, a cinema, and a sweetshop near my home.

Well, it did happen. I stood there for a last look round before leaving. Where did our cottage stand, and whereabouts was the pond from which we caught newts and tadpoles? The tall old pear tree which grew by the roadside and produced large iron-hard fruit? The lovely old farmhouse still stood there, probably because of its historical background, and further along the road stands a timbered period cottage, holding its own amidst modern structures.

I drove off, mentally bowing to progress, but with a deep sigh for what is gone for ever.

On my way home I slowly drove along the lanes leading to the school I attended for the first two years of my education, and looked in vain for the field footpaths which used to make the two-miles walk so much more interesting, especially during haysel, and when the hedges were a mass of wild roses, and the scent of a bean field in flower rivalled the sweetness of the ripening hay.

When we were children my sister and I often walked those two miles to the village shop to spend our pennies, and were helped in our choice of sweets by the elderly, kindly shopkeeper. The shop was a source of interest to us, with its large advertisement of

Mazawattee Tea depicting an old lady in lace cap and shawl, sitting beside a little girl dressed exactly the same as the old lady, even to the spectacles. Needless to say, nothing much of my memory of the shop remained.

I went on my way again, this time heading for the famous Hethel Thorn tree. At last I was seeing something which had not changed in all those years, unless it had grown larger and seemed to have more props supporting the boughs.

So much food for thought, in my journey back to youth, when the sun always seemed to be shining in those long, lovely summers.

The Village Pub (i) Marsham White Hart 1890's

I was born at Marsham White Hart, eighty-two years ago; my grandfather, Mr Christopher, was landlord there for thirty-two years. My mother remained there after her marriage.

In my very early childhood there was no rail service between Norwich and Cromer, and all mail and fish carts came by road, stopping at the White Hart to change horses on either journey. I can remember coming downstairs in the mornings and seeing the kitchen table covered with fish and crabs crawling round the floor.

I remember the White Hart was a very busy house, and pigs were killed into the house every year to supply bacon and ham. I used to be terrified as a child coming down in the morning and seeing the great fourteen- or fifteen-stone pigs hanging there. Cheeses were bought whole and kept in a large bowl covered in butter muslin, which was kept moist with beer.

There were two big local events during the year. One was when the men from a nearby farm, each with his wife and one child came for a wonderful supper, all hot. I can remember seeing the kitchen coppers full of vegetables and dumplings. Then there was the tithe payers' dinner, also hot.

I can remember when performing bears came on the road and stayed in one of the stables; their trainers slept with them. The bears had half a loaf of bread each and some beer for their supper.

In the summer months many social parties came from Norwich to spend the day at Cromer, and they would always stop on both journeys for a meal while the horses were rested. My grandmother would always keep great tins of gingerbread ready for the parties.

On a Friday night there used to be a carrier; I think he came from Alborough, and he used to bring the Norfolk News. My grandfather would read out the news to the customers in the bar, and they used to keep very quiet, not a word spoken. They had to rely in those days on just the one paper of the week; there were no daily papers and no telephone or anything of that sort.

My grandfather retired when I was ten years old. Although I was born in a Public House, I was very strictly brought up and was never allowed in the public part when customers arrived. I always had to attend church twice a day on Sundays.

The years passed on, and my father was called up for service in South Africa. During this period my grandfather died, and so did Queen Victoria. The death of the Queen was made known by the tolling of the death bell about eight o'clock in the evening—there was no other communication in those days. Everybody was very upset, and all wore mourning—black and lots of crepe, even the children.

(ii) The Regulars Mulbarton 1890

'My dad,' said the old man, 'liked his glass, and every evening, regular as clockwork, he'd go with his cronies down to the pub. They allus sat on the same bench, back to the window; my old dad in the middle a-sucking his pipe, one fellow on his left a-pulling of his moustache, and the other always stuck his legs right out and rested his head on the window sill. Blow me if they didn't allus look the same way. My dad would order a pint, and the tankard would be passed from one to the other till it was finished. That happened every night—far as I can remember.'

Christmas Day in the Workhouse West Beckham 1914-18

I remember Christmas Days in the Workhouse, some of the happiest of my life. No, I was not an inmate, although at the time, from six years until ten years I was quite sure that to be one was to be as happy as myself.

My grandfather, grannie and auntie were respectively Master, Matron and Assistant Matron at a small county workhouse at West Beckham, near Holt, about four miles from my home. To me it was Heaven and Fairyland all in one, and I certainly saw it through rose-coloured spectacles.

On Christmas Eve my brothers, sisters and I were bundled into big coats, shawls and rugs, the trap was loaded and we were loaded up. It was a back-to-back cart, and we soon learnt that it didn't pay to look downwards on the road—that was asking to feel sick. The gas was put out, the door locked, and off we jogged with father riding on his bicycle beside us. We rumbled along in the darkness with only the candle-lit carriage lamps and father's oil bicycle lamp.

At last we were there and up the drive to the House—out of the trap stiff and cold and into the warm 'Lodge', as the entrance hall was called. We were welcomed by 'Old Alder' at the desk and the strong smell of oil lamps.

Then down the flagged passage to the 'Octagon', the centre of the House, around which my grandparents had their quarters. Great swags of evergreen were everywhere strung across the passages. These had been made by the old men by threading twigs of ivy, laurel and holly on string.

The sitting room door would open, and there was granny in black, with a cap of velvet and lace—grandad behind her, tall, benign, with a beautiful silver beard, and auntie in her pink uniform and white apron and cuffs.

When we had been thawed out with hot cocoa and mince pies it was off to bed—bed being beds all over the place.

Then it was Christmas morning and the children singing carols actually outside the bedroom door. Then to look at our presents. There were five of us, so there was only one present each, but always a new dress and pinafore to wear on the great day.

Our presents duly presented and appreciated and breakfast over, it was time to go with granny on her Christmas rounds with a present for everyone—sweets for the children, tobacco for the men and tea and a cap and apron for the old ladies. To me everyone seemed happy and in my grandparents' special care.

Across to the Infirmary, just separate from the House, with gifts for the bedridden and to see the decorations in the wards. Then to the big kitchen to watch the preparations for dinner, which was served in the dining hall to all the able-bodied. Families were allowed to sit together, a great treat for them which I was too young to appreciate. The great range which cooked the great rounds of beef, and the great cauldron in which the yellow football-sized Christmas puddings were cooked, fascinated us, especially when they were hauled out of the copper on a pulley. My grandfather, father and the porter put on their aprons, sharpened their knives and carved the beef. Potatoes, greens and gravy were got ready, and then we were allowed to run backwards and forwards to the dining hall carrying loaded plates. Men and women were allowed a glass of stout or beer and the children lemonade. I remember one old man who put meat, pudding and vegetables all together and then ate them. He told astonished me that anyhow 'it mixed when it got down'.

Then to granny's back room, where we and all the staff that could be spared sat down to our own Christmas dinner of turkey and pudding. There was no time to linger, as we must hurry back into the dining hall and help (?) Anderson the inmate carpenter build a stage for the evening entertainment.

Tea for everyone in the dining hall—stacks of dripping toast made at the kitchen range, mugs of strong tea and sweet biscuits, which once again we helped to serve. This was our opinion, but I have never known if it was that of anyone else. When tea was over it was upstairs, wash, comb hair and don the new Christmas dresses, with instructions on how to keep them clean and how to behave during the evening. We certainly wouldn't risk being turned out of the Hall, with everyone in there and only long passages lit with oil lamps outside it.

At last seven o'clock and the concert began. I loved the decorated stage, even the 'institution' smell was exciting to me. The children performed; we did our duet and dialogue; the staff did a patriotic tableau, and everyone sang the war songs 'Tipperary' and such like. It was the time after the Interval that I loved most of all. Many of the inmates had spent much of their lives at the House and had their one or two songs which they always sang. They needed no asking, and grandfather would call on them in strict rotation.

Blind Jinny 'The Old Arm Chair'; Crutches Hardingham 'The Miners' Dream of Home'; Alden 'The Death of Nelson'; and so it went on, everyone singing the chorus.
It seemed to me to go on for ever, but at last grandfather would say a prayer and goodnight. Everyone went to bed, the doors were locked and we returned to the back room for supper. There seemed masses of food and lots of people, but I never remembered going to bed, only waking the next morning and realising that it was all over and I had to face the journey back to a cold, empty house. I was sure none of my friends had had such a marvellous Christmas. When my grandparents retired and we all went to their home the following Christmas, how we missed all the fun and excitement of Christmas in the Workhouse!

Going down the Common Southery 1915

Going 'down the common' is a vivid memory for me. Not that Southery Common was a vivid place. In fact, it was mostly black earth bordered with grass and weeds, just a wide drove that continued into the fen from Common Lane.
Years later I learned that certain areas of arable land adjoining the drove were let to villagers and known as 'Common Rights'. This was of no interest to me in my younger days, as I went 'down the Common' simply because my schoolmate lived there.
For many months of the year the footpath beside the dyke was very slippery. Only farm workers with waggons, tumbrils and animals used the drove, where there were many deep holes filled with thick, black mud—known locally as 'slub'—into which the horses sank to their bellies. During the dry periods of summer, clouds of soot-like dust arose from the animals' feet, dulling the weeds and grass; and to ride in a cart was reminiscent of a monster switchback where one wheel went down into a hole while the other went up over a mound and people and packages were tipped from side to side.
The soft spring green of the corn crops, quickly growing to five feet or more in height, soon turned to a wonderful harvest gold. One 'spring-blow' and the bright potato tops became dull and dingy. Immediately after harvest time in went the horse-drawn

ploughs, and the black earth again stretched darkly across to the green line of the Brandon Bank—(little Ouse)—intersected by the leaden-grey water of the dykes dug in rectangles to drain the fields. Only the yellow bricks of the homesteads glowed in the sunshine of winter, while the dark outlines of the few fruit trees were lost against the backcloth of the fen.

The brightest things, because of or in spite of the mud and dust, were the immaculately groomed horses, their shining coats highlighted by the ripples of strong muscles, the harness leathers smooth and supple, the ribbons bobbing and the brasses gleaming; while the workmen's leather 'lace-ups' and 'buskins' were polished to a mirror-like finish each morning.

Until floods washed it away my friend's house was much like its neighbours, spaced along the sides of the drove, beyond the dyke which was crossed by a plank. It consisted of 'two up and two down', with a wash-house adjoining. There a sizeable family was brought up by hard-working parents with kindness and joy and respect for others.

Often I carried home a sweet, moist wholemeal loaf, home-made from wheat which the mother had gleaned in the surrounding fields and had had milled in the village. Never has bread tasted so good. Sometimes I was given a banty's (bantam's) egg if I helped Lily to look them up. The bantams and hens found their own nesting places behind the wood stack, in patches of nettles or by the dyke-side. Freely the poultry roamed the yard, scratching for corn, cracked maize and insects among the grit, and coming into the hen-house to roost at night. Those brown eggs, collected in a tater-skip (potato basket) contained dark orange yelks (yolks) and thick whites such as only 'free-range' birds can produce.

Until the age of six I had lived in a Northamptonshire town among business people, where I learned the King's English. My family then 'flitted' to Southery, and very soon I acquired a second language—that of the Fen Folk. Instinctively I knew when and where to use it, keeping the language of my parents for use among the 'half sixes', as the Fen folk called the élite of the village.

One afternoon on an excursion 'down the Common' I saw two tumblers (tumbrils) meet. The drivers stopped to give the old hosses a breather and pass the time of day. Big-ears-me listened:

'Hello, bor, that hev bin a nice day.' 'Yis, that hev. I just bin up town to git the hoss collar from Tom's cuzz, we'll be tatering next week.' 'Shorely they een't fit to dig yit?' 'That they are, bor. Will you give us a hand?' 'All right, my old feller. I'll hev to git on, it's nearly time the hosses were hoom.' 'So long, me old bor.'

I had love and respect for these Fen folk, some being alive today, for they made me 'one of their ilk', while most strangers who moved to Southery remained 'furriners' for life.

People

Life with Grandfather Reedham 1910

The centre of my childhood revolved around three people, my grandfather, grandmother and Abbie. Abbie White lived quite near us and we spent every minute of our play time together. I believe he shared with me the love of my grandparents and all the adventures the boat yard and the river provided in my grandfather's company.

Abbie and I were of the same age so went to school together. We also played truant together many times—the old river front provided such good hiding places for this.

I don't think we did too badly at school considering our main interest was to get out and home to my grandfather. We three were always together whenever possible and we were frequently referred to as old Jimmie Hall and his little 'mawther' and that boy of 'Niffler White's'. It was all pleasure to be with my grandfather, he was the most wonderful man I've ever known. Mark you, he made us work, and when there was a wherry 'pulled out' on the boat yard, he made us fetch and carry for him, and woe betide us if we were gone too long, or brought the wrong tool back.

I'm sure the weather must have been very different in those days. It seemed we could always bank on lovely warm evenings. This was the time my grandfather would take us up the river in our own little boat. Sometimes we would be out late, and watch the sun go down and the moon come up. We even used to believe the red ball of the setting sun used to hiss as it appeared to sink slowly into the river.

Sometimes we would be accompanied by another old man, Charlie Elvyn. He would ask my grandfather to take him up the Chet which was a good place for eels. There he would put out his eel trunks or 'bat' for eels all night, in which case my grandfather would fetch him back at sun rise.

My grandfather made up all sorts of lovely stories about the creatures that inhabited the marshes and river bank. We really believed that the numerous dragon flies that fluttered over the reeds were fairies, they flew so gracefully and were so beautiful. I think there must have been thousands of toads and frogs in the 'roads'. These we didn't much care for until my grandfather pointed out that they had beautiful golden eyes and a ruby in their foreheads. This is quite true, their eyes are golden and they do have a jewel, perhaps it was to make up for them being a little bit ugly. The 'roads' was a mass of glow worms at night and we used to think it was to light the late travellers home, and that the big brown beetles that blundered about in the summer twilight were little policemen that kept things and creatures in order.

My grannie was a good gardener. Little Willie Hindle had a conservatory and as he cut down his geraniums each year he would throw the waste pieces into the river, which the tide would bring up to our garden the following day. We would fish them out of the river and my grannie would get them to grow so we always had a window sill full of flowers and shaded by white lace curtains. We never went into town but always for walks sometimes with both my grandparents but mostly just my grandfather. Of course in those days we had our Sunday clothes even 'pinnies' and these were always kept for Sundays only. Every night my grandfather heard me say my prayers, and he and I went to bed early. Sometimes he would tell me stories of his boyhood or he would sing songs, some of which I think he made up for I have never heard them since or anywhere else. Grace was also said before and after every meal. At the end of my prayers at night my grandfather always gave 'Thanks for the Day'.

My grannie used to do a lot of washing for the parson and the one job I hated was having to take bundles of clean linen back to the Rectory some time early in the week. My only comfort was that Abbie always came with me on this two mile walk and that I had the best little wheel barrow in the business. My grandfather made Abbie one too but his was painted red while mine was blue.

I went into service when I was 14, and it was at this time my grandfather died suddenly and the world really toppled about us. I felt my childhood was far away and I had grown into a woman at 14 in a few weeks. I had so much to do when I went home on half days—I tried to do all the things my grandfather had done.

Village Characters Gimingham 1920's

Characters abounded. Old Mrs Creed the village gossip, who, it was said 'had made her wall right bent with allus a'leaning on it' in her anxiety to miss nothing that was going on. Poor old Keggs who was never without a flower behind his ear, and had never done a day's work because 'he never got no further than Thursday'. Billa the postman, a man of leisurely habits: his legs rotated so slowly as he rode his bicycle that it was a daily miracle that he didn't fall off. Dick the member of the choir (unrobed), who had never worn a collar or tie in his life, but kept an especial stud for Sundays.

The Reason for the Nicknames Southery 1915

I passed the cottage where Charlotte 'Bellman' lived. I well knew that her surname was Osler but because many people in Southery were named Osler, and many had inter-married and were related, practically all were known locally by a nickname to which they answered quite happily and without rancour.

The Cranky Lord Costessey 1890

Great-grandfather Gunton lived in an old fashioned house at the Brickfields, on the verge of Costessey Park, very near Costessey Hall where Lord and Lady Stafford resided. Lord Stafford made imitation diamonds and seemed to the ordinary village folk to be decidedly cranky. He was quite old and Lady Stafford was young and beautiful. He had about forty clocks in the Hall and an old villager named Billy Pank was ordered to go to the Hall each day to wind the clocks.

Rich Aunt Matilda Sprowston 1920's

Aunt Tilley was my mother's cousin once removed but I imagine financially even more so. I often heard my mother refer to her and Uncle Fred as comfortably off and having money in the bank. I was sure it was the one at the bottom of the garden which extended to about two acres beautifully laid out with an orchard which had some much talked about Dr Harvey's apples.

To me Aunt Tilley was a round lady a bit like Mrs Noah in my Japhet's annual. She had rosy cheeks, always wore pink or mauve jumpers, a black pinstripe skirt and in the mornings a black apron with a large pocket like a kangaroo in the front. It was wonderful how much it could hold, always plenty of string or bass for tying up stray ends in the garden. Her loose change for paying the tradesmen was kept in a chamois leather bag with a draw string at the top, a bunch of keys jangled somewhere underneath.

Uncle Fred was tall, always in a good Harris tweed suit and cap (from Greens on the Haymarket in Norwich). I don't know if it was always the same one—they did wear rather well I believe. He never seemed really to have to work. He pottered around in the garden and looked after the pony. Some days the pony would be harnessed into a small cart and he would drive me back into Norwich with him, we would go to lots of small cottages and collect what he called the rents. (That was why he didn't have to work I thought!) All those ladies in their little houses giving him money but they all seemed quite pleased to see him. They smiled and called him Sir. If we didn't go towards Norwich we would go for a trot along Blue Boar Lane. But this wasn't always very successful as mother's Uncle Charlie lived in a small cottage on the corner and he had a donkey and cart, and Uncle Fred's pony would not go past the donkey—class distinction I expect—so we had to turn round and come back.

We arrived one day at Aunt Tilley's to find a large aerial had been erected half way down the garden. Aunt Tilley had a new wireless with a large black horn. William, the gardener's boy, was called in from the garden; the daily woman left her bucket and brush and Agnes left the dusting, and we all gathered round it to hear the news. I don't remember many programmes but do recall very clearly Uncle Mac calling out the birthdays and the 'Hello Twins'. Uncle Fred wasn't keen on it and when he got bored he wouldn't bother to get up to switch it off, but would throw a large yellow duster into the horn which just left us with muffled whispers. Aunt Tilley was the one who enjoyed it most for the racing results because she loved a flutter on the gee-gees. She would jump up and down and tell us her horse had won in nearly every race. When I was older I found out that she always backed nearly all the horses for a small amount, so she always had a winner—I can't guess how much she lost.

The house seemed quite large to me as a child. It actually had three outside doors which made it rather special. The front door was very seldom opened, the side door was for visitors and the back for tradesmen.

The stair carpet was always covered with grey stuff. I think they called it drugget. It always seemed such a pity to me to have such nice carpet and then cover it over with that horrible grey stuff. But that was the reason for my mother's visits. She often had to mend the wretched stuff. She sewed nearly all day, darning the clothes, sides to middling the sheets, making curtains and loose covers for the chairs. You see, she was what they called handy with her needle. For this we received a very nice lunch and not so much in cash as in kind. I often wondered why mother took the large push chair when I was quite old enough to walk, but after she had finished for the day, Aunt Tilley would provide the spoils—a few eggs, a basin of dripping left over from the Sunday joint, fruit and vegetables. These were carefully packed into the push chair, with room left for me if I got tired and wanted to ride. A large bunch of flowers topped the lot. When we arrived home mother would take the push chair right indoors to unload it. She had her pride, you see, and the neighbours just thought she had enjoyed her day out at the big house.

Events

The 1912 Flood

One of my early childhood memories is of the disastrous weather of the summer of nineteen hundred and twelve.
My brother and I had whooping cough and in August were sent, in charge of a nursemaid, to Bacton to recuperate. We had rooms at Bromholme, an old house facing the Abbey ruins. It rained persistently every day and was cold and windy with rough seas. The only toys we had were spades and pails which were of no use to us. I have no recollection of seeing the beach but remember a village shop where we were taken to buy sweets, clad in sticky black oilskins and sou'wester hats. For hours we stood at the window of our sittingroom watching the rain falling in the pond the other side of the road.
Our landlady's son told us he had been 'palking'. At that age I had no idea what that meant but connected it with pigs. Later I found out it meant pulling driftwood and other things from the sea brought in by the high tides.
Our one desire was to get home. The day my mother came to fetch us our nursemaid put us both in the push chair and walked along the road to meet the horse and trap. She was as anxious as we were to get away.
A few days after we got home my father drove us to Coltishall to see the floods there. The river had burst its banks and the road bridge on the Norwich road had been swept away and flood water was lapping round the houses in the main street.
The floods were very bad in Norwich too as the river there had burst its banks at many places. I have some picture post cards still of men rowing boats in the Norwich streets. An uncle in Norwich sent them to me as all children in those days had a post card album.
In our village I remember the miller taking men and big boys to the top of the mill, where there was a balcony, to get a good view of the acres of land under water. It was a disastrous year for both farmers and farm workers alike. Sheaves of corn floated in the

fields. Some corn was never cut and the harvest dragged on all through the autumn.

Also, needless to say, the sea air did not cure our whooping cough. I remember my mother saying it was with us until the next spring.

There have been many changes along the Norfolk coast. The village shop, where we bought our sweets, is no more and the pond has been filled in. However, I am pleased to see Bromholme still stands and has not been a victim of ever increasing road widening. Whenever I see it I remember two small children, with their noses pressed to the window, watching the relentless rain making 'ducks and drakes' in the ever growing pond on the other side of the road.

The 1914-18 War (i) Aylsham

The schools broke up for the Harvest Holidays in August 1914 with the cloud of war hovering over the country. On 4th August I remember coming from school and seeing people congregating in the Market Place outside the Post Office (now the International Stores) and the Black Boys, waiting for the latest news. The hushed silence was strangely ominous, for even we schoolchildren realised that fathers and brothers would be leaving to fight the enemy.

In 1916 our homeward train was brought to a standstill between County School and Foulsham. Out popped our heads from the darkened compartment to find out the reason and the guard told us that a zeppelin was circling overhead, probably waiting to follow our train into Norwich. We actually saw the zeppelin which left later on as if to go towards the west, and then our train crawled into Foulsham station. There we were, cooped up in the semi-dark, frightened by the thuds of falling bombs, then cheered by the tea sent down from the village. An invitation to have supper and rest in a nearby house where one of our schoolgirl friends lived was accepted, and we were there until the early hours of the morning when a porter came to tell us the train was leaving.

I still have somewhere, a book with the names of all the householders in Hungate Street, numbers of inhabitants, digging tools they possessed, and if they had cellars. This was in case of invasion by the Germans so the Parish Council would know how many people had to be evacuated. In the event of this happening we were to go to the railway bridge at the junction of Hungate Street and Yaxley's Lane and taken by wagon towards Dereham. My father had this district to do and he put me down to help to drive the horses. At this time there was only one cottage on the east side of Hungate Street past Palmer's Lane, and a Mrs Hunt lived there who had a callender which we liked to see working.

(iii) Hevingham

One night when the zeppelins came over, it didn't seem too good, but we heard, with relief, in the morning they had only killed one cabbage in a field at Hevingham.

The 1939-45 War (i) Cromer

It was war-time; evacuees all over the county; blue-bulbs to light the railway carriages, making knitting for Britain difficult; soldiers in the holiday hotels and drilling on the promenade; sentries challenging us in perfect B.B.C. English as we made our way home after serving in the Y.M.C.A. canteen, then inviting us to come and show our identity cards in a variety of accents from all parts of the country. The beach was out of bounds, barbed-wire everywhere, naval guns on the cliff and A.R.P. posts everywhere. I was sitting in the train at Norwich station when bombs dropped on the line in front of us in the first of many raids on the city. One week there was no drinking water in Norwich and we commuters brought a supply from home each day. A static water-tank stood where had been Curl's large store and many Norwich homes were destroyed. We had several small but frightening raids on Cromer but one night in 1942 the central pattern of the town was changed. I saw the effect next evening. The church with shattered windows was surrounded by the debris of Church Street and uncanny noises came from inside the building as the organist tried to play the damaged organ.

(ii) Hainford

In our big house at Hainford there were terrible difficulties blacking out so many windows.

We had bombs falling all around us, flares and parachutes dropping, planes crashing, including American airmen, and the house was often machine-gunned, bullets penetrating the roof, one even entering a top-hat box, going round the inside without touching the hat.

(iii) Brandon

'There's a War On'. This was the often given reason for everything lacking—toys, eggs, bananas, clothes, Fortune Chocolates, Stork Margarine, lights—an endless list. Most of all, though, there were no Daddies around.

When war broke out in 1939 I was one year old and, after a year in which I remember Mother as something like a Land Girl, we found ourselves in a tiny haunted flint cottage amid the Brandon pine forests.

Only a cart-track, miles long, impassable in midwinter, led to Ickburgh Fields. In summer the way was glorious with wild tough-stalked scabious and red campion, poppy and marguerite, and the air was heavy with pine-scent. They were unrationed luxuries! Mother worked picking fircones for a few shillings a bag and sometimes I would go with her. In mild weather the freedom, peace and solitude were sublime, but in the winter of 1942 the snow, although ethereal in its beauty, made us prisoners in the cottage. My toes became frost-bitten and I had to suffer scalding bread poultices. Whose breakfast was requisitioned for that, I wonder? Water we carried from the well up the hill, and the privy down the path was the usual hole and bucket delight. Candles, our only lights, had to be shaded carefully from the malicious eyes of 'Jerry' circling overhead at night in evil-sounding craft. At three I knew which were 'ours' and which 'theirs' by the tone of the engine.

When the time came for me to go to school, we had to move a little closer to civilisation and so went to Hilborough. We stayed a week or two next door to the school, where we had sickening, watery wartime rice pudding every single day, then moved in with a stone-deaf old lady who had to turn up her little wireless to an ear-shrivelling volume to hear the news.

An aircraft crashed in the meadow next to the cottage and smouldered, hell-like, for several interesting days. Such events provided entertainment, for there wasn't much, although occasionally there were village dances at which Mother played her violin. The band wasn't much like Glenn Miller, but all the same was greatly enjoyed by all. Once, later in Northwold, I was allowed to go. Dressed in dark blue velvet (probably made over from something else), with long dark hair loose and straightish, I conquered the hearts of the American servicemen there. They begged Mother for a photograph of me which, alas, she didn't have. They must have missed their families badly, I think, for they were always exceptionally kind to us children and their generosity kept us in comics and chewing gum. We loved them.

We moved yet again, to Northwold and a farm overrun with children and kittens. We invaded the barns, took over the little garden for our own patches of parsley and Wanda and streamed through the village on Sundays, girls dressed in Sunday best with flower-bedecked straw bonnets, returning later with them filled with purple orchis, golden primroses or heavenly, stolen lilac. We danced round the maypole there, too, and I remember such a patriotic fervour among the villagers that not only did we all wear red, white and blue ribbons in our hair on victory day, but I knew fourteen girls christened Margaret after Princess Margaret Rose!

Other brief memories flood in—of Father occasionally arriving, gloriously handsome in the days when it was the fashion for men to be handsome, laden with Mickey Mouses and threepenny bits and once—oh joy—a length of tartan for a skirt for me. Of the Church Army Camp where Mother battled with a scrubbing brush and filthy floors while I picked harebells on the heath, of bathing in the Blackwater and having a real lady teach me 'Incy Wincy Spider'. Of Mars Bars and Camp coffee and slab cake and Marmite and Craven A cigarettes. . . .

My grandfather made beautiful toys for me fit to last for generations and although my own small daughter now has many of them for her own, she can never have the special memories which attend each one of them. She who has had her fill of toys, clothes, eggs, bananas, chocolates and butter, never mind margarine, and who cannot imagine night without lights, nor life without her adored Daddy, will she remember, I wonder, her first six years with such poignancy and affection?

(iv) Great Moulton

With only a small weekly ration of sweets, a friend and I thought of a plan to beat sweet rationing. We went to the local chemists shop and bought some liquorice. Much to our disgust it wasn't quite like the sticks we bought from a sweet shop, and it also had undesirable after effects. I remember that our next door neighbour was constantly thinking up cake recipes minus this, that, or the other that we were short of during the war, and the look of triumph on her face when she produced the fatless or sugarless masterpiece. When any party was advertised in the village the posters would have B.Y.O.G. at the bottom, and we all knew it meant bring your own grub.

(v) Wisbech

'This is the end of England as we know it,' said my husband as the air-raid warning filled the air on Sunday September 3rd 1939. But for some months of the phoney war of that year things went on much the same, except that my husband joined the Local Defence Volunteers and spent some nights out every week. Also our top floor was used as a look-out post for firewatchers as it had access to a very high roof which overlooked the town.

Soon things began to tighten up and the coast was barred to the public. When the war began in earnest, the scare was on that the Germans would land on the marshes near our town, and the Council arranged evacuation of children to Canada and America for those who were willing to let their children go. After days and nights of heart-searching we decided to let our only daughter go with some of her friends. They sailed from Scotland, and after a week we were awakened early one morning by the telephone to

say that the ship had been torpedoed but that our girl had been taken by a tanker to Glasgow. There she was being fitted out with clothes as they had escaped only in pyjamas.
After that we decided that home was best.

The Women's Institutes (i) Blofield 1918

What a good thing came from a few ladies first meeting in a drawing room to start a Women's Institute in our village. Now it is the oldest Institute in Norfolk. To mark its 50th anniversary the Institute gave Blofield a village sign.

(ii) Hardingham 1918

I remember the day in 1918 when our Women's Institute was formed. A meeting was arranged to appoint Officers and a committee. I was unable to attend as the doctor was calling to vaccinate my baby. My mother attended and told me she had been put on the committee and she had put my name down as a member. My mother was one of the keenest most loyal members. She wore her W.I. badge wherever she went by bus or train. She was rewarded for this. One Saturday she went to Norwich and was going to the Headquarters in Davy Place for a rest and a cup of tea. A crowd was gathered outside. They told her Queen Mary was expected and only those wearing a W.I. badge could go inside. She went in and found other members forming a line for Queen Mary accompanied by the Duchess of York, to pass along. Mother was thrilled and said the Queen smiled at her.

(iii) Langham 1932

I am a founder member of our W.I. It started in Langham three miles away. My sister and I used to walk to the meetings and that meant we had to cross a very muddy field to get on to the main road. We used to take a pair of goloshes with us, put them on to cross the field, then hide them in the hedge till we returned to repeat the process.

(iv) **Hardingham** 1968

I remember taking part in the Norfolk Federation of Women's Institutes Jubilee Pageant at the Royal Norfolk Show in 1968. I, with two other members, wore outfits of fifty years ago. Mine was a black satin blouse and skirt, a black necklace, and a black straw hat with grey pompoms. We rode round the Grand Ring in a vintage car. The people were waving and clapping. We rode past the Royal Box in which Queen Elizabeth the Queen Mother sat. We felt like Royalty ourselves.

Conclusion

'I have read somewhere,' wrote one of our contributors, 'that the memories of one's youth make a soft cushion for old age. Well, I have a very fine soft cushion.'

'God gave us memories,' quotes another, 'that we might have roses in December.'

We said in the Preface that we were not trying to draw conclusions from the facts presented, and we have not attempted to decide whether they were good old days, or bad old days in the past. But one conclusion we just have to draw: good or bad, or a mixture of both, the past is something that everyone enjoys remembering. Talk to anyone about the subject of this book, and in all probability you will trigger off the reply: 'Well, *I* can remember. . . .' Well, can *you* remember? If so, why don't you start writing your reminiscences now?

List of contributors to the 'I Remember' Essay Competition, 1970, and the Women's Institutes to which they belong

Mrs J Baird	North Walsham and District
Mrs J M Balls	Cromer
Mrs L E Bevan	North Walsham and District
Mrs J M Bird	Taverham
Mrs M Bird	Holme Hale
Mrs M E Brown	Stanhoe and Barwick
Mrs M Botwright	Southrepps and District
Mrs D Carter	Alburgh
Mrs M A Chettleburgh	North Walsham and District
Mrs M Chilvers	Great Ormesby
Mrs G Clarke	Sprowston
Mrs C Coller	Shipdham
Mrs G J Colman	Fincham and District
Mrs M Cooke	Thurne with Clippesby
Mrs Z Cunningham	Terrington St Clement
Mrs B Davey	Thurne with Clippesby
Mrs A Dennes	Neatishead, Barton and District
Mrs E Farrow	Sandringham
Mrs V Fenn	Hellesdon
Mrs M Gentry	The Runtons and District
Miss B Gilbert	Blofield
Mrs J Gilbert	Aldborough and Thurgarton
Miss B M Goffe	Keswick and Intwood
Mrs L S Goulty	Little Plumstead
Mrs W Green	Briston
Mrs K M Grix	Caston
Mrs I Hardwicke	Surlingham
Mrs M Hill	New Costessey
Miss E Hopper	Field Dalling and District
Miss G M Hudson	Blakeney
Mrs B C Jackson	Bunwell and Carleton Rode
Miss G M Kendle	Swaffham
Mrs G N Kett	Caston
Mrs G Lovick	Colney, Earlham and District
Mrs W Lown	North Walsham and District

Mrs O G Mason	Ludham
Mrs W P Melluish	North Walsham and District
Mrs M B Mingay	Strumpshaw and Lingwood
Mrs H Moy	Hardingham
Mrs O L Pearson	Stalham
Mrs C M Quantrill	Aslacton and Great Moulton
Mrs L C Radford	Hainford and District
Mrs M M Reynolds	Keswick and Intwood
Mrs I M Richardson	Sprowston
Mrs A Robbins	Keswick and Intwood
Mrs E Roberts	Hellesdon
Mrs P Rook	Cromer
Mrs W Rout	Bradwell
Mrs L E Runnacre	Aylsham
Mrs P Rix	East Winch
Mrs M Schamp	Knapton and Paston
Mrs I Scott	Antingham and District
Mrs K Sigee	Hemsby
Mrs O M Skoyles	Aylsham
Mrs G Smith	Great Witchingham, Weston and District
Mrs V Spalding	Aylsham
Mrs A Stubley	Knapton and Paston
Mrs H Turner	Knapton and Paston
Mrs M E Ulrych	Thompson
Mrs D M Webb	Hilgay
Mrs G Whiting	Spooner Row
Mrs H Williams	New Costessey
Mrs M M Wilson	Pentney and West Bilney
Mrs E M Wiseman	Swaffham
Mrs L Yarham	Cantley and District

Index of places referred to in the text

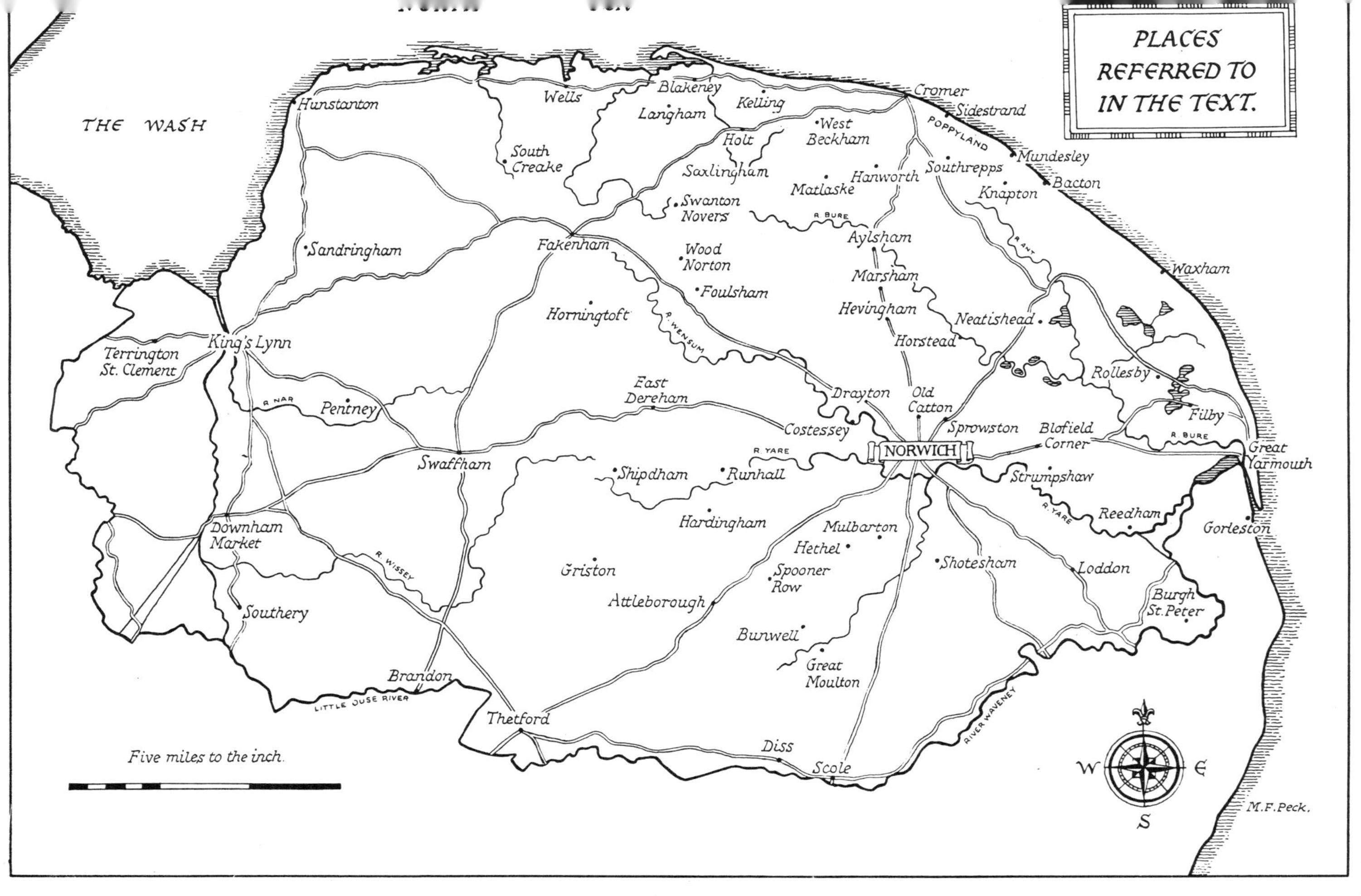
PLACES REFERRED TO IN THE TEXT.
THE WASH
Hunstanton
Wells
Blakeney
Kelling
Cromer
Sidestrand
POPPYLAND
Mundesley
Bacton
Langham
Holt
West Beckham
South Creake
Saxlingham
Hanworth
Southrepps
Matlaske
Knapton
Swanton Novers
R. BURE
Aylsham
R. ANT
Sandringham
Fakenham
Wood Norton
Waxham
Marsham
Foulsham
Hevingham
Horningtoft
Neatishead
R. WENSUM
Horstead
King's Lynn
Terrington St. Clement
Rollesby
East Dereham
Drayton
Old Catton
Filby
R. NAR
Pentney
Sprowston
Blofield Corner
Costessey
R. BURE
Great Yarmouth
R. YARE
NORWICH
Swaffham
Shipdham
Runhall
Strumpshaw
R. YARE
Reedham
Hardingham
Gorleston
Downham Market
Mulbarton
Hethel
R. WISSEY
Shotesham
Loddon
Griston
Spooner Row
Attleborough
Burgh St. Peter
Southery
Bunwell
Great Moulton
Brandon
LITTLE OUSE RIVER
RIVER WAVENEY
Thetford
Diss
Scole
Five miles to the inch.
W
E
S
M.F. Peck.